Building Wealth One House at a Time

JOHN W. SCHAUB

McGraw-Hill

New York Chicago San Francisco Lisbon London
Madrid Mexico City Milan New Delhi San Juan
Seoul Singapore Sydney Toronto

The McGraw·Hill Companies

1 2 3 4 5 6 7 8 9 0 DOC/DOC 0 9 8 7 6 5 4

ISBN 0-07-144835-7

This publication is designed to provide accurate and authoritative information in regard to the subject matter covered. It is sold with the understanding that neither the author nor the publisher is engaged in rendering legal, accounting, or other professional service. If legal advice or other expert assistance is required, the services of a competent professional person should be sought.

—From a Declaration of Principles jointly adopted by a Committee of the American Bar Association and a Committee of Publishers

McGraw-Hill books are available at special quantity discounts to use as premiums and sales promotions, or for use in corporate training programs. For more information, please write to the Director of Special Sales, McGraw-Hill Professional, Two Penn Plaza, New York, NY 10121-2298. Or contact your local bookstore.

This book is printed on recycled, acid-free paper containing a minimum of 50% recycled, de-inked fiber.

This book is dedicated to conscientious landlords who invest their time and capital to provide affordable housing.

And to the dedicated volunteers, staff, and homeowners of Habitat for Humanity who are working together to eliminate poverty housing.

Contents

Contents

Introduction

Tens of thousands of ordinary people have made millions of dollars investing in the most humble of real estate investments, the single-family house. I am one of them, and I have a unique perspective because I have helped thousands of others make their first million by buying houses.

Buying, renting, and selling houses is not only highly profitable but also helps people in your community. By treating people fairly, you develop a reputation for helping others, and many will refer to you their friends and family when they need to sell, buy, or rent.

By providing a supply of decent, affordable housing, you help young families live near their work while they save enough to buy their own homes. When you buy a house from someone who needs to get rid of it, you relieve him of a burden. When you sell a house and finance it, you often can help someone buy their first home.

Many ordinary people are now millionaires not by winning the lottery but by systematically buying houses. Rather than put their trust in a company pension plan or the government, they have taken control of their financial destiny. By doing what they have done, you can change your life become financially independent, and be in control of your financial future. It takes less time than you think. Simply follow the advice in this book.

HOW INVESTING IN HOUSES CAN MAKE YOU RICH

You don't need a lot of education to make a lot of money in real estate. It's not that complicated. In fact too much education can cause you to overthink and develop analysis-paralysis.

The one thing that keeps most people poor is the fear of buying that first house. Some of my most successful students have taken a year or more to buy their first house. That's fine, as long as you buy it. The second house will be easier, and as you get better at it, you will really enjoy the process of finding and buying a good deal.

MY FIRST HOUSE

It's not even important that your first house is a great deal. The first house I bought I paid retail price for and made a 20 percent down payment. The good news is that I could rent it for a high enough amount to pay the expenses and pay the loan. The reason it has been one of my best investments is that I still have it. Thirty years have past, the house is paid for, and it is worth several times what I paid for it.

An investor with a doctorate in finance would never have bought that house, and he would have never held it for 30 years without refinancing it. He would have been concerned with his rate of return, his lack of leverage, and his running out of depreciation. He would have never turned a $7,000 investment into more than $300,000, not counting the rent that was collected for 30 years and will continue to be collected for the next 30 years. The annual rent I collect today is about twice my entire down payment 30 years ago.

Building wealth one house at a time does not require a lot of education, money, or even time. It does require one thing—that you buy a house and hold it until it makes you some serious money. This book will show you step-by-step how you can build your fortune one house at a time.

1

HOW BUYING ONE HOUSE AT A TIME CAN MAKE YOU WEALTHY

Everyone knows something about houses. Ask them, and they will tell you their opinion about what house prices are doing; they even may tell you about a good deal they just missed. Most people agree that a house can be a good investment, yet only a few actually make money investing in houses.

Houses are not complicated, and they're not scary. Their performance is predictable. They produce income when rented, and house rents have a long history of increasing. Likewise, house prices have increased at an average annual rate of roughly 5 percent for about as long as we can measure. Some years houses go up at a much higher rate, and occasionally, they do not go up at all and even drop in price. Some houses rarely drop in price, and those are the ones you want to buy.

When houses are not going up in price, you will make your best buys. The old adage, "You make your money when you buy," has a double meaning when buying houses.

First, you have to buy a house to make money. Just looking won't make you rich. Second, you can make thousands of dollars in profits every time you buy if you buy a house that someone else does not want.

WHY HOUSES ARE YOUR BEST INVESTMENT

After 32 years of investing, I still buy houses instead of apartments or shopping centers. Why? Houses make me more money *with less work* than any other investment.

There is a common conception that commercial buildings or apartments are less work. I've owned both, and I can tell you that this is not true. The tenants in apartments and commercial properties often come and go. Every time they leave, the property will need work. Every time they move, you need to find a new tenant. In short, apartments and commercial property require ongoing work.

Commercial buildings are rented by tenants who often have lawyers and accountants. This will cost you money and time if there is a dispute during or after the rental. If you rent to a "big name" tenant, it is likely that they will pay you less than market rent because they have a name and you want them in the building.

If you have the misfortune of having a commercial tenant filing for bankruptcy, you may have a tenant who does not pay rent or renegotiates a much lower rent. If the tenant abandons the lease, you can hire a lawyer and sue him, but if the tenant goes broke, you won't get paid.

You want to buy property that attracts good tenants—tenants who will pay rent and take care of your property. You want to buy a property that you can rent to tenants who are not great negotiators and who need you more than you need them.

A side benefit of buying and managing houses is that you can help people sell houses they don't want anymore. You can rent houses to people who need a place to live, and when you sell, you can help people buy their first house. You can solve big problems by buying a house that an owner can't afford and that is ruining that person's credit. Even when you sell for a profit, you can help a family buy their first house. These are all profitable and rewarding experiences.

HOUSES ARE DIFFERENT FROM OTHER INVESTMENTS

Houses are unique investments. You can rent them to provide income, but their value does not depend on that income. Even an empty house can make you money. It will appreciate as much as a full one.

The value of other investment real estate, such as apartments or commercial property, depends on the amount of income it produces. If you rent an apartment or office space for below-market rent, it will be worth less money. An empty house is worth as much as a full one.

Houses are much safer investments for several reasons. First, there is less money involved. You often can buy a house with a small down payment, so you have less at risk. Lenders routinely will lend more against a house than any other type of property.

Next, there are more buyers for houses than for bigger properties. If you need to sell in a hurry, you can—if you offer a house at a good price. Third, houses rent faster and have fewer vacancies. Apartment vacancies often run 10 to 20 percent, whereas house vacancies rarely exceed 5 percent. Commercial properties sit empty for months and even years at a time between tenants. You need a lot of cash in the bank to survive a long-term vacancy in a large building.

WHEN YOU BUY, YOU ARE DEALING WITH AN ANXIOUS SELLER

When you buy a house, typically you are dealing directly with a homeowner who is in a hurry to sell. If the homeowner had plenty of time to sell, then she could wait for a retail price. When you decide to sell any real estate in a hurry, you will have to discount the price to sell it quickly. Learn this lesson: Never put yourself in a position where you have to sell in a hurry.

When you buy commercial or apartment property, you are buying from another investor. You may still be able to negotiate a good deal, but often you are dealing with someone who is an experienced negotiator. He might be better at this than you are. When you buy from a homeowner, you have more negotiation experience and, therefore, the advantage. You will not buy unless you can make a good deal.

WHEN YOU SELL, YOU WILL GET A RETAIL PRICE AND ALL CASH

More important, when you decide to sell a house, *sell only to a user*. You want to sell to someone who really likes the house, because if they really like your house, they will pay a retail price.

Now, for the really important part! When you sell a house to an owner occupant, that person usually can get a loan for nearly the entire purchase price; in some cases the loan will be for more money than what the buyer pays. You will receive all cash when you sell.

If you want to finance the sale to generate interest income, you have that option. There are always buyers who need help with financing, and often you can sell at an even higher price if you will agree to finance the property for a buyer who cannot qualify for a bank loan. However, if you want the cash to reinvest in another house or just to spend, you can have it.

A disadvantage of selling an apartment building or commercial property is that the buyer will be another investor. This investor will negotiate to get the best price and terms that she can.

THE PROBLEM WITH MOST INVESTMENT PROPERTY

The buyers of investment property are other investors. Like you, they want to buy for less than the property is worth and would like to buy with a low down payment. Unfortunately, banks will only lend a portion of the selling price, often 60 or 70 percent. Often the buyer will not have enough for the down payment, so the deal falls apart, or the seller must agree to finance part of the price.

Investment property can experience large swings in value as the economy changes. An empty office building or commercial building will sell for a small fraction of what it cost to build.

A well-located house will appreciate at a greater rate than an average property and will not suffer the dramatic drops in value common in commercial properties during business recessions.

DIVERSIFICATION BRINGS SAFETY AND HIGHER PROFITS

Not all houses perform the same as investments. Higher-priced houses may jump more in price during a boom, but lower-priced houses rarely drop in price. It costs a certain amount to buy a lot and build a starter house in your town, and that price is constantly increasing. This supports the lower-priced houses in the market.

A major advantage of investing in several houses rather than one big apartment or office building is that you can diversify by investing in different price ranges. By owning both less expensive and more expensive houses, you can have the safety of the lower-priced houses and the upside potential of the higher-priced ones.

WHEN AVERAGE ISN'T AVERAGE AT ALL

Read reports of prices booming or busting with a little skepticism. Remember that the headline writer's job is to sell newspapers, and a spectacular headline is more likely to get him a bonus.

When the press reports that the average price of a house rose or dropped, that report is often an exaggeration of what is really happening in the market. The average typically will include the more expensive houses, which are more likely to stop selling when the market cools off.

There is no national house market or national trend for real estate. Although some factors, such as interest rates, the economy, and national security, have national implications, even these affect different housing markets differently.

Housing markets are local in nature. The Southeast can be booming while the Northwest is experiencing a recession. In one town, a neighborhood may be appreciating while another is declining in value.

Changes in interest rates will have a more profound effect on house sales in towns where there are a lot of first-time buyers than in a town where many buyers are retired and pay cash for their homes. A threat to national security may drive prices up in areas considered safer while depressing prices in areas perceived as higher risk.

HOW AVERAGES CAN MISLEAD

Suppose that last month four houses sold in your town, and they sold at these prices: $100,000, $150,000, $150,000, and $400,000. The average price of a house sold that month was $200,000. If the following month four other houses sold at $100,000, $150,000, $150,000, and $200,000, the average price of a house sold in your town that month would be $150,000.

Just because the average price of a house sold in your town dropped from $200,000 to $150,000 in one month does not necessarily mean that houses are decreasing in value. It simply means that fewer expensive houses sold that month.

Averages include houses that you don't want to own. Track the prices of houses in neighborhoods that you want to own. Research what a particular house sold for new and compare it with its resale price to get a real appreciation rate for a neighborhood that interests you.

HOW TO LEARN AND ANTICIPATE THE REAL TRENDS IN YOUR TOWN

To learn how houses have performed as investments in your town, identify several houses that have sold recently in neighborhoods that you think would be a good place to invest. Research what those houses sold for in previous years. You can find this information in your public records. In the past, this usually meant a trip to the courthouse, but now this information is often available online.

Now calculate how much these houses have increased in value per year on average. Continue to track these houses, and add others to your research as you discover other neighborhoods that you think have potential. This information will help you to identify neighborhoods with a strong history of growth, and you will begin to learn the values in your town.

Neighborhoods and towns are dynamic. They are changing constantly, and you need to become a student of that change. Neighborhoods and towns change like seasons change. If you are paying attention, you can feel, see, and recognize the signs of change early in the cycle. This will enable you to be among the first to buy in a market changing for the better and among the first to sell in a market changing for the worse.

FACTORS THAT AFFECT HOUSE PRICES IN YOUR TOWN

Changes in Population

A growing population will create an increasing demand for housing. If your town is growing in population, then your prices probably will outperform the national average. If your town is losing population, your prices may not increase without inflation and could decline if the loss in population is permanent. People make real estate valuable. Without people, land has little value except to hold the earth together.

Changes in population in nearby communities will also affect your market. If a nearby city is growing rapidly, then it will have a positive effect on your market.

Demographics

When populations change, it's not just in number. As new people move into your town, they will have new needs and demands. If they are young working people moving to your town because of jobs, they will need houses that will house children and will want to be near schools and parks that cater to family activities.

If the newcomers are retired, then they may want to be near medical centers, entertainment facilities, and restaurants. The Bureau of Census is a valuable source of information about age, income, family size, and education levels.

Government Regulation of Developers and Builders

As populations boom and overwhelm roads, parks, schools, and other public facilities, it is typical for the existing population, through the local government, to react and take steps to slow growth. The result is often a dramatic increase in the cost and time required to develop land and build new houses. It makes existing housing much more valuable.

Inflation

Inflation is increasing prices as a result of an increased supply of money and credit. Picture 50 college students in a room. You show up with tickets to a popular sold-out concert that you will sell to the highest bidder, but only for cash. The sales price would be limited to the amount of money in anyone's wallet at the time.

If before you held the auction you gave everyone in the room $100 in cash, then it's pretty predictable that the amount that they would be willing to pay for the tickets would be higher because they had more money. If you would allow them to bid any amount they wanted and would agree to finance the tickets for a year at 6 percent interest, the price bid would be higher still.

The federal government can stimulate economic activity by increasing the amount of money we all have. It does this by both increasing the amount of money in circulation and increasing the amount of money the government lends to banks at relatively low rates. The banks, in turn, can lend this money to consumers and businesses, thereby stimulating buying.

Inflation will drive up the prices of all commodities, including land and house prices. Investing in houses protects you against inflation because both your house prices and rents will keep up with inflation. A leveraged house will allow you to make a dramatic profit with inflation.

Compare prices of commodities that you buy every day with the prices of houses in your town and the rents that they produce. Table 1.1 shows some numbers from my town.

Compare the numbers in your town. The relative value of these items has not changed much. Inflation of the currency has changed the amount of money it takes to buy these items.

Some people are confused by the fact that the prices for some items seem to be cheaper, such as computers. When a new product or technology hits the market, it will be priced high in its early years until the demand increases. This increased demand allows manufacturers to increase production to levels where prices fall because of the economy of producing thousands or millions of the same product. Another factor that can drive down prices is competition. Nothing inspires competition like extraordinary profits.

Table 1.1 The Effect of Inflation on Your Purchasing Power

Year	Commodity	Price
1970	Gasoline	$0.25/gallon
1970	Chicken	$0.23/pound
1970	Haircut	$1.25
1970	New midrange Chevy	$2,000
1970	New three-bed, two-bath 1,400-square-foot home	$20,000
1970	Rent for the same house	$140/month
2004	Gasoline	2.50/gallon
2004	Chicken	2.00/pound
2004	Haircut	$20
2004	New midrange Chevy	$20,000
2004	New three-bed, two-bath 1,400-square-foot home	$200,000
2004	Rent for the same house	$1,400/month

In inflationary times, you want to invest in assets, such as houses, that protect you from the tremendous loss in purchasing power that inflation causes.

Inflation hurts the investor with cash in the bank. With $100,000 in 1970 in my town, I could have bought five brand new homes. With the same $100,000 in 2004, I could buy one-half of a house. If you plan on being here 25 years from now, that same house may cost you $2 million.

Inflation also hurts those who invest in fixed-income investments. If you bought an annuity or held a mortgage with payments of $500 a month in 1970, you would have had enough income to buy a new car every 4 months. With the same income in 2004, it would take you 40 months of income to buy the same car.

Everyone can predict the future. Unfortunately, the future usually pays no attention. If the next 25 years is anything like the last 25 years, the investor with cash in the bank or holding fixed income securities or mortgages will be hurt, whereas investors in real estate will benefit.

Interest Rates and the Availability of Credit

There is almost always a supply of buyers who want to buy houses. When they can qualify for a loan, they will buy. The interest rates affect how much a buyer can borrow, so lower interest rates make it possible for many more potential buyers to qualify for a loan.

When banks are running over with deposits and need to make loans, they become creative and will find a way to help marginal borrowers qualify for loans. Often, independent mortgage brokers will originate loans that are then sold to banks.

Low interest rates and easy credit will fuel a hot real estate market, causing prices to rise dramatically and allowing some buyers to qualify for a loan that they will be unable to repay. These runaway credit markets typically are followed by a wave of foreclosures as the marginal borrowers give their houses back to the lenders.

Cycles in the Economy

When jobs are lost, the economy suffers, and real estate prices, especially the prices of higher-priced properties, can drop. There was a report during a recession in the 1980s about a woman in Texas who had to sell her $180,000 property for $140,000, losing $40,000. Reading further, I learned that she had paid only $80,000 when she bought the house but could have sold it for $180,000 at the top of the market. What she considered a $40,000 loss really was a $60,000 profit.

Buy when it's hard to sell, and sell when everyone wants to buy. There are cycles in housing prices. Although the overall trend is definitely up, there will be opportunities to buy at discounted prices from homeowners who need to sell quickly and from speculators who purchased more than they can afford to carry.

Assess your market conditions before you buy. Always look for good deals because you can find them in any market. When the market is hot and appreciating at double-digit rates, buy only properties that you can afford to carry. Often interest rates will be low, so you will be able to borrow on great terms.

When it is easy to buy, buy at bigger discounts. Look for builders and banks who have property they will sell cheap, and negotiate both a good price and good terms.

HOW 5 PERCENT A YEAR AVERAGE APPRECIATION CAN MAKE YOU RICH

How can an investment that goes up 5 percent a year make you rich?

If you buy a house that will produce income, your return will be much higher than 5 percent. If you borrow most of your purchase price, your rate of return could be 50 percent or more.

Suppose that you bought a house worth $120,000 and paid a retail price. If you borrowed 80 percent of your purchase, you would need a 20 percent, or a $24,000, down payment. If the rental income would just cover the monthly payments, and the house appreciated at 5 percent the following year, 5 percent of $120,000 is $6,000, a 25 percent return on your $24,000 investment.

If you learn how to buy a house at below-market prices and then finance even more of the purchase price, your rate of return increases considerably.

Suppose that you bought the same $120,000 house for $110,000 and were able to buy it with a $10,000 down payment. You still get the

FIGURE 1.1 The amazing result of owning one house.

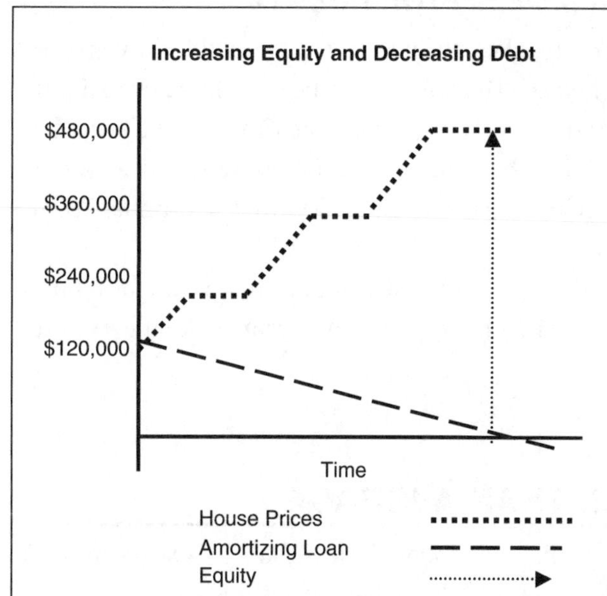

FIGURE 1.2 The rule of 72.

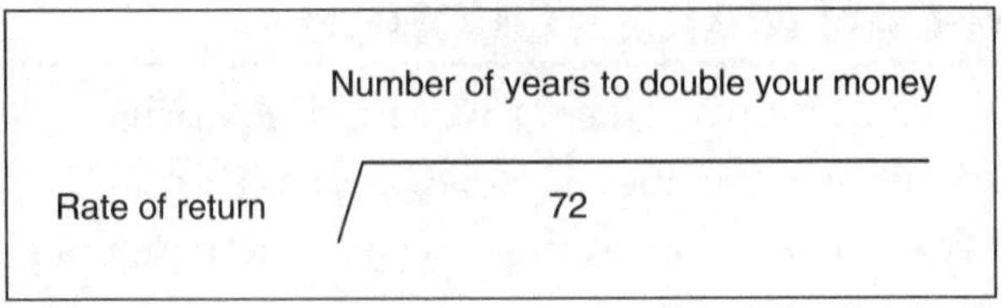

	Number of years to double your money
Rate of return	72

5 percent on the full $120,000, so you will earn $6,000 on a $10,000 investment—not accounting for the $10,000 profit you made when you bought the house.

The power in buying real estate on leverage comes in the following years as your profits increase at a compounded rate. The next year your house would be worth $126,000 and go up another 5 percent, or $6,300. The amount the house value goes up increases each year; at the same time, you are paying off debt (see Figure 1.1).

Real estate fortunes are made by buying houses and by then financing them so that you can afford to hold the house until it is free and clear of debt.

DOUBLING YOUR MONEY–THE RULE OF 72

Do you know how long it takes an investment to double in value if it goes up 5 percent each year? The answer can be calculated by using the rule of 72, which states that you can calculate the time it will take to double your money by dividing the compounded rate of return (the interest you would earn on a savings account at a bank) into the number 72 (see Figure 1.2).

Thus, 72 divided by 5 equals 14.4. It will take 14.4 years for a house that increases in value at the rate of 5 percent a year to double in value.

$$72/5 = 14.4 \text{ years}$$

DOING BETTER THAN AVERAGE

You want to buy houses that will double in less than 14.4 years. You can shorten the time it takes significantly by doing two things:

1. Learn how to buy a house for less than its retail price. The 5 percent average appreciation is based on retail prices. When you learn to buy below retail, your rate of return will be significantly higher.
2. Buy a house in an area with better than average appreciation. Some of my houses have averaged 12 percent a year appreciation. At that rate, they double about every six years. If I can buy a house at a below-market price that will double in value in six years, I can shorten the amount of time it takes me to turn my 10 percent down payment into $300,000 to four years or less. Look at these results.

Market value	$150,000
Your purchase price	$135,000
Your down payment	$ 13,500
Your loan	$122,500

The house appreciates at 12 percent a year and doubles in value in six years.

Market value in six years	$300,000
Loan balance in six years	$120,000
Your equity in six years	$180,000
Net return on your down payment	$180,000/$13,500 = enough[1]

This does not include cash flow produced by the rental income.

BUYING WITH NOTHING DOWN

Read the classic book, *Nothing Down,* written by my student Robert Allen. Robert was a young real estate agent when he took my seminar in the mid-1970s. He bought a number of properties and then wrote about his experience.

You can buy property with nothing down. If you doubt that, look for a property in your town that has been empty for six months or more. Make the owners an offer with nothing down, and agree to take responsibility for the property and begin making them monthly payments. When you own an

[1] Using the Rule of 72, the compounded rate of return can be figured by asking how often $13,500 doubled in six years. The answer is 3.67 (13,500 × 2 = 27,000 × 2 = $54,000 × 2 = 108,000 × 0.67 = 180,000). It doubled then about once every 1.6 years (6/3.7). To calculate the compound annual rate of return, divide 72 by 1.6 and the answer is 45 percent.

empty property for months and months, the prospect of someone else taking care of it and making you monthly payments looks good. I know!

Some of the property that you can buy with nothing down, you may end up selling for nothing down to the next adventurer. There is a lot of property that is only attractive to people with no money. As you acquire more money, you acquire better taste in property.

Sometimes great properties are available with nothing down. It's not the property that has the problem; it's the owner. Find an owner who has a big problem that he cannot solve, and you may have found an owner who will sell to you with nothing down.

A local lender foreclosed on a property that was occupied by several tenants and a pit bull. After the dog chased the bank representative off the property, the bank sold the property the next week at way below market and nothing down.

WHEN YOU BUY WITH NOTHING DOWN, YOU OWE IT ALL

When you buy a property with nothing down, you owe the full amount of your purchase price. The terms you get on the money you borrow are more important when you borrow the entire amount than when you buy with less leverage. If you can't make the payments, you will not own the property long enough to make a profit.

You need a plan to generate enough income to repay the loan, or you will soon lose the property. Buying with high leverage is risky business. It is a great way to acquire property when you are starting, but it's like driving a car at a high speed. You need to be totally focused on what you are doing, or there is a good possibility of a wreck.

Another student of mine purchased more than 100 houses—really—the year after he took my class. He bought many of them with nothing down because he was starting out with almost no money.

Unfortunately, he bought faster than he could find good tenants. Eventually, he sold most of these properties for little or no profit because he could not afford to make the payments on a lot of empty houses.

If you buy more than you can manage, nothing down can lead to nothing left.

BUYING 100 HOUSES–ONE AT A TIME

Other investors have accumulated far more than 100 houses following my advice to buy them one at a time.

Buy one, rent one, then and only then look for the next deal.

By using this strategy, you will learn management at the same time you learn to buy. Ask yourself this question, "If I begin buying houses aggressively, will I make a better deal on my first five houses or the last five houses that I buy?" If you are learning from the experience, you will make much better buys on the last five houses.

2

BUYING THE RIGHT HOUSE

Now that you can see how buying houses can make you money, it's time to get into the specifics of which house you should buy. Having a plan and buying a house that fits into that plan will help you to meet your goals in a shorter time. Most people who buy real estate do not set out to buy a particular property. They just look at everything that is for sale and hope to find a good deal. You can do far better by targeting a house that will make you the most money.

Not all houses are created equal. Some houses will appreciate more; some will produce more cash flow because they will attract better tenants; and others will require more maintenance and have higher expenses. No house is perfect, but you can increase your profits significantly when you target a certain house to buy. Buying houses without a plan can still be profitable, but buying with a plan will make you more money sooner.

BUYING DIFFERENT HOUSES FOR DIFFERENT REASONS

An advantage of investing in houses is that—over time—you probably will buy more than one. Owning different houses in different neighborhoods allows you to diversify. Some houses will produce more cash flow, and some will appreciate more. Owning houses of different sizes, different ages, and different prices makes your "portfolio" safer than owning one larger property because your income and expenses are spread over many properties.

When you begin to invest, naturally you will focus on properties that produce more income. Less expensive "starter homes" will produce more cash flow. These homes often are built in tracts where all the lots are the same size and all the houses are about the same size and look a lot alike. They are around 1,000 to 1,200 square feet in total size, with small bedrooms and few frills.

These houses are in high demand and appreciate at an above-average rate because few new ones are being produced. Most new houses are larger, more elaborate, and more expensive. The more expensive house typically produces more profit for the builder.

Starter houses rent well and generally rent fast. During hard economic times, tenants often downsize to these houses to save money.

The next step up on the investment ladder is a slightly larger house in a little better neighborhood. There are several reasons to buy these houses as investments.

1. This house is more likely to attract a longer-term tenant because it has more space and better neighbors. You can buy this size house in a neighborhood that is predominantly owner occupied. Owners take better care of their property than most landlords, so the neighborhood will look better and attract better looking tenants.
2. If you have other income, pay taxes, and want to reduce your taxable income, you can do this by investing in slightly more expensive houses. A more expensive house will produce larger capital gains but less net rent in relation to its value.

Table 2.1 Making more, buying higher-priced houses

Asking Price	Your Purchase Price	Rental Income
$100,000	$ 90,000	$ 8,000
$150,000	$135,000	$10,000
$200,000	$175,000	$12,000
$300,000	$260,000	$15,000
$400,000	$350,000	$18,000

The tax rate on capital gains income is always significantly lower than the tax rate on ordinary income, such as rental income. If you can buy a more expensive house at a bigger discount, then you are using the tax system to your advantage to earn larger profits and pay less in taxes. Study the example of houses that you can buy in different price ranges shown in Table 2.1.

These prices and rents represent no particular market, just the principle that as you buy a more expensive house, you are able to buy at bigger dollar discounts. Also, notice that the rents do not increase in direct proportion with the price of the house. The lower-priced houses produce more rental income as a percentage of their value. If the income is important to you, start with the lowest-price house in your town that is in a decent neighborhood.

A high income taxpayer would have more after-tax profit if he bought a more expensive house because more of the profit that the house produces would be a capital gain and less would be rent.

THE RIGHT NEIGHBORHOOD

Buyers and tenants are attracted to neighborhoods that are quiet, safe, well maintained, and populated by responsible people. Good neighbors make a good neighborhood. Buy houses in neighborhoods where you feel safe and comfortable talking to the neighbors. The tenant you are likely to rent to probably will look and talk a lot like the people who already live on the street. You need to be able to relate well to your tenant, so you should relate well to the neighbors.

Good neighbors are attracted by many factors, including geography. High ground, the right exposure, and proximity to roads, rivers, lakes or oceans, hospitals, work, and schools are all factors that affect desirability—and therefore value. Study the geography in your town and learn why certain areas are more popular and therefore more valuable.

Schools have a significant effect on neighborhood values. Get to know which schools in your areas are the most desirable. Become knowledgeable about which schools are improving and which are becoming less desirable. Watch for information about planned new schools and possible redistricting. Both tenants and buyers will want to live in the best school districts that they can afford. Often new schools are popular and attract both good teachers and good students.

Buy in the best neighborhood that you can afford. A house in a better neighborhood will make you more money. If you are beginning with little, then still buy in the best neighborhood that you can afford. As you build more cash and cash flow, you will be able to afford to move up a notch in location.

BUYING THE RIGHT-SIZED HOUSE

When you buy a house that you want to hold as an investment, you want it to be attractive to good tenants—tenants who will stay a long time and take good care of your property. You want to rent to a tenant with long-term potential, not someone who is constantly on the move. Tenants with the long-term potential typically are coming out of another house where they have accumulated furniture and lots of other stuff. You want to buy a house that has enough space for such a tenant to live in comfortably.

The overwhelming majority of home buyers prefer at least a three-bedroom, two-bath house. Renters have the same preferences. If you buy a smaller house, you will have to compete at a disadvantage with all the three-bedroom houses in your town for rent. There is not a big difference in price between a two-bedroom and a three-bedroom house, but there is a big difference in demand. The three-bedroom house will rent faster and stay rented longer. Buy houses that have three or more bedrooms.

Larger houses containing four or five bedrooms are common in communities with larger families. I don't recommend these larger dwellings as a preferred house, but they can be as profitable when there is demand for them as rentals. You would learn about this from your research before you start making offers.

Garages or basements are big pluses both when you sell and when you rent. Storage space is important to everyone. Again, the cost of buying a house with a garage or basement is not that much higher, but the garage or basement is a big advantage when you rent or sell.

Yards are a big selling point to families with children and pets. In my town, most tenants have both, so having a fenced back yard makes it easier to rent or sell. Most tenants will maintain a yard but rarely will improve one. Look for houses with average-sized yards for your town. A large yard may scare off tenants who see it as too big of a job. The lack of a back yard that kids can play in is a definite disadvantage. A nearby park can compensate for a small yard.

SOME HOUSES ARE TOO BIG OR TOO FANCY FOR INVESTMENT

While you can argue that once you own the lot and the house, a few extra square feet costs little money to add, in reality, every square foot you add to a house does cost you. The fixed costs such as taxes and insurance increase with size and value, and so does the cost to maintain the house.

An investment house should be big enough to attract a normal-sized family with their belongings, but not much bigger. While I would feel safe living in any house that I own as an investment, most of my stuff would not fit in them.

I would be comfortable living in any of my rental houses because the neighborhoods are quiet and the neighbors are friendly. However, the investment houses are smaller and lack some of the luxury items that you may be used to in your own home.

Buy a house that is functional and well located, and then keep it in good operating condition. Don't buy a house with a lot of fragile items such as fancy wallpaper, trim, elaborate landscaping, and so on. The tenants won't take care of it, and it will not look as good in a year as it does today. Avoid houses with high-maintenance frills such as pools and hot tubs. They are expensive to maintain, and only a small percentage of the buying and renting population will pay the price to have one.

While there is no "right sized" house, as houses get larger and more expensive, they become more expensive to operate and less profitable as investments. Beware of buying a house you really like unless the reason you like it is the great neighborhood.

IT'S THE LOT THAT GOES UP–NOT THE HOUSE

Every day a house is wearing out and becoming obsolete. It's the lot that is becoming more valuable. To make the most money, you want to buy the best lot that you can, and hopefully that lot will be improved with a house that you can rent to a decent tenant while you wait for the lot to make you some serious money.

Some lots are better than others. Avoid lots on busy streets or strangely shaped lots. Even corner lots are not as valuable as interior lots. With a corner lot, you have to set the house back from two streets. This leaves you with a big front yard on two sides but an unusually small back yard. Although corner lots are good for model homes, most owners would rather have a back yard.

The location of the lot is the key to how much money you will make in the long run. The advantage of buying several houses for investments is that you can target three or four neighborhoods in your town that you feel will appreciate at better than average rates. If you buy in all three or four, then you are likely to hit a couple of hot areas that will give you a larger than average profit.

NEIGHBORHOOD LIFE CYCLES

Neighborhoods are changing constantly. When they are new, most neighborhoods are almost totally owner occupied. As the houses age, some owners will rent their houses or sell to investors who will rent them. The rental houses are rarely maintained as well as owner-occupied houses, and they have a negative effect on values. Sometimes the neighborhood will become completely owned by landlords. You can spot these streets by a lack of pride of ownership.

If these neighborhoods are in good locations, eventually owners will begin moving back in and buying bargains that they can fix up and live in. When this happens, property values will start to appreciate rapidly. Study the neighborhoods that interest you to see if you can establish where they are in this cycle. Buy in an area that is improving, and you will make more money.

THE RIGHT FINANCING

Your ability to borrow and to make down payments will change with time. You may start with little money and no credit. You can still buy a house. You will need to find a nontraditional source of financing, such as owners who will sell you their house and finance the purchase for you.

I have never borrowed money from a bank to buy a property.

When I started investing in real estate, I was working as a commissioned real estate salesman with no history of producing income and no predictable income. The banks would not make me loans to buy property because I had no demonstrable way to pay the loans back.

As I began to buy houses and accumulate both equity and cash flow, the bankers began courting my business. By then I had found both faster and cheaper sources of money. To this day, I have never borrowed money from a bank to buy a house.

Other investors, sellers of property, and private lenders provide a source of both down payments and long-term financing. In Chapter 6 on financing you will learn to use all three.

The right financing will allow you to buy a house with the down payment that you have and afford the payment each month. Ideally, you will be able to borrow on a long-term, fixed-rate loan. With a fixed-rate loan, you get to keep the profits as your rents increase. With a variable-rate loan, the lender will make more money as interest rates rise.

A long-term loan is important to you if you plan on holding a house for investment. The longer-term loan will have lower payments. Low payments make this a safer investment. Avoid short-term loans. You may have to sell or refinance to pay them off. If interest rates are higher when you have to sell or refinance, you may end up paying a much higher interest rate or selling at a discount.

As the economy changes, you will borrow at different interest rates. When rates are the highest, you will make your best buys. When rates drop, you will be able to borrow at low rates and refinance your high-interest-rate debt, increasing your cash flow.

THE RIGHT CASH FLOW

The cash flow a house produces depends on both its financing and its ability to produce income. If you finance the house with a long-term low-interest-rate loan, then you have won half the battle.

The other half of the challenge is buying a house that will attract good tenants and will have average or below-average operating expenses, such as taxes, insurance, and maintenance.

Before you buy, research the property taxes and learn if they will change if you buy the house. Property taxes often increase when a property is sold. Contact a local insurance agent and get an estimate of what it will cost to insure a house of the construction and age you are considering.

Estimating the maintenance cost is difficult. A well-designed, well-built, and well-maintained house should be cheaper to maintain. An experienced home inspector or friendly building contractor can look over a house and give you advice about how much maintenance that house is likely to require. Don't ask someone whom you might hire to do repair or maintenance work to inspect the house. That's like asking your barber if you need a haircut.

THE RIGHT TENANT

We all have little personality quirks. It bothers me when people don't take care of things. If I loan you something, I'd like you to return it—and return it in good condition.

This can be a problem when you loan someone a nice house to live in, and then they don't take care of it. Yes, they pay rent to live there, but that does not give them the right to abuse your property.

The good news is that if you buy the right property, you can attract tenants who will take good care of it. In 30 years, I have had hundreds of tenants—and only a few bad ones. One measure of your success as a landlord is the number of tenants you have to evict, that is, legally force to leave your house. I have had to evict only six tenants in 30 years. The others have paid as agreed and taken reasonable care of the property.

This record with tenants is not just good luck. I learned many of my lessons the hard way—by making expensive mistakes. Hopefully, you won't have to repeat the same mistakes to learn the lesson.

One of my first investments was a brand-new nine-unit apartment building. It was a beautiful property, and I thought that I would own it forever—until I met the tenants. I thought at the time that there would be a certain efficiency in having nine tenants living close together. Collecting the rent should be easy: just drop by on the first of the month and pick up my money.

The first month I dropped by to find only one tenant home. There were plenty of cars in the parking lot, but after I knocked on the first door, no one else would answer. It took me nine visits to sneak up on all nine tenants, and after all of that effort, I still got several stories and promises to pay rather than actual rent.

Here I was, a young, poor landlord who needed every rent check from that building to make the mortgage payment. The tenants saw me as a wealthy landlord, but the truth was that they drove better cars than I did. To add insult to injury, many had bigger TVs and fancier stereos, yet they would not pay me the rent.

It was a cultural difference. These tenants came from a culture where if you could talk the landlord out of the rent, it was a good thing. I learned that I wanted to own property that would attract tenants who felt that paying the rent on time was a good thing and would feel some remorse if they were late.

THE RIGHT TENANT–NOT TOO RICH AND NOT TOO POOR

Your first reaction might be that a tenant can't be too rich. The problem with a rich tenant is that she won't stay long. She will buy, and you will have a vacancy again.

Tenants certainly can be too poor. People are poor because they don't have any money. There may be a lot of good reasons why they don't have any money, but if they don't have money, they will not pay the rent.

I divide potential tenants into three broad groups. Those with too much money, those without enough money, and those with just the right amount of money. Obviously, I want to buy a house that the last group can afford and wants to rent.

The amount of money that good tenants earn varies from place to place. Most of my tenants have hourly or commission jobs and earn between two and three times the base wage in my town. Often there is more than one wage earner in the family. They often have enough income to afford to buy a house if they would just pay off their bills and save up a down payment. Those two obstacles are insurmountable for many tenants.

Study your market. Don't rent to people at either end of the income range in your town. Aim at tenants who make enough money to afford your rent and their other normal expenses. Later you will learn about tenant screening and selection.

BUYING THE RIGHT FIRST HOUSE FOR YOU

You want your first house investment to be a success, especially if you are married. You increase your chances of success by buying close to where you live. It may not be in your neighborhood, but it should be as close as possible. Most people live only a few minutes from an area of right-sized and right-priced houses.

When you target an area close to where you live, you can spend time in that neighborhood and really learn the market. Walk the streets and talk to the neighbors. Tell them that you want to buy a house in their neighborhood and ask them if they know of anyone who wants to sell. You are complimenting them on living in a nice neighborhood. You will be surprised at how helpful they will be.

Call on every house for sale and for rent until you know the market well enough that you can walk down a street and give a price and rent for each house. Use a range: It would sell for between $140,000 and $160,000, or it would rent for between $900 and $1,000. Now, when a house comes on the market, you will know what it is worth and what it will rent for. You can confidently make an offer, knowing that if the owner accepts, you have made a good deal.

3

FINDING GOOD DEALS

Now that you know the price range and size of the house you want to buy, you can begin looking for opportunities. This can be overwhelming because there are lots of properties for sale. Focusing on certain neighborhoods and specific types of properties in those neighborhoods will help you to sort the houses you want to research and then to make an offer.

SOURCES OF OPPORTUNITIES

A great thing about buying houses for investments is that there is an unlimited supply of opportunity. Every day new ads appear in your newspaper. Every day people put their property on the market. Every day people's lives change unexpectedly, and they decide to sell their house. Every day is full of new opportunities.

One of my teachers, Warren Harding, encouraged me to look for good deals close to where I lived and worked. He advised never to drive the same street twice. Instead, drive down different streets in different neighborhoods, and you will constantly see new opportunities. Real estate opportunities are everywhere, yet some investors drive for hours or even go to other states trying to find greener grass. They drive past or fly over thousands of opportunities near where they live.

Out-of-town management can be an expensive adventure. I know first hand: I've owned investment properties in 10 states. Today I only own property in my town. Owning property close to you allows you to stay on top of the management or to manage it yourself. Even more important, you know your market and can buy when there are buying opportunities and sell when the market is hot.

Most buyers look at properties listed for sale. In my experience, houses that are real opportunities are not on the market for sale. They are not listed, and there is no sign in the front yard.

When you can identify a house that an owner wants to sell and that is not listed, you have less competition from other buyers. Here are my top sources of opportunities for investment homes:

1. *Empty houses.* An empty house is costing somebody money every day. In addition, it is a source of worry and work for someone. Look for empty houses, and contact the owners. If the house is empty, knock on the neighbor's door and ask if he knows where the owner has moved. If that fails, look up the neighbor's phone number and call him. The neighbor does not like an empty house next door, especially if it is not being maintained. Neighbors can be a valuable source of information. The owner may be a lender who has foreclosed or an heir who has inherited the property.
2. *Houses that need work, especially in nicer neighborhoods.* Houses in disrepair stand out, especially on a good street. Some people are just poor housekeepers, but more often, they are short of money to repair the house. Occasionally, the house is rented to a tenant who is not maintaining it. All these situations signal potential profit.
3. *Out-of-town owners.* While you cannot see this from the street, you often can find an owner's name and address in the public records. When you spot an empty house or one in disrepair, look up the owner. Often this can be done on the Internet. If not, go to your

county courthouse and ask for help in looking up a property's owner. While you are there, ask how to find out if there are any mortgages or liens against the property, and read those. You can learn what the current owner paid and what she owes.

4. *Landlords who are not maintaining their property.* When you see an occupied house in disrepair, knock on the door and ask if it is for sale. If it is rented, the tenant typically will tell you and may even give you the landlord's name and phone number. If the landlord is out of town, he may be more than willing to sell. You can tell the tenants that if you buy it, you would be willing to fix it up and maybe rent to them. Sometimes the tenant is the problem, and sometimes the problem is the owner.
5. *For sale by owners (FISBOs).* Many owners try to sell their property without the help of a broker. Some of these owners do not have enough equity to pay a broker, and you can buy their house simply by taking over their payments. Other sellers may own their property free and clear and be willing to finance the purchase. Still others have had bad experiences with brokers and may be anxious to get rid of a house that is a problem to them. Their problem may be your opportunity. Before you go to see their house, research what they paid for it and what they might owe on the public records. Ask them the questions listed in Chapter 4. Don't waste your time and energy going to see a house until you are sure that it is an opportunity that you want to buy.
6. *Real estate agents.* Although some of my best buys have been from agents, they are a seasonal source of deals. When the market is hot, they don't need buyers, so you won't get many calls. When the market cools off, they have more sellers than buyers, and they will call you. Ask a lot of questions when they call to qualify the house. They will try to sell you anything they have listed. Don't waste your time unless you smell opportunity.
7. *Lenders.* Like agents, lenders are a seasonal source of good buys. When the economy softens and lenders foreclose on many loans, they need buyers and will be cooperative in selling you properties at wholesale prices. When the market is hot, they have few foreclosures and don't need buyers (see Chapter 12).

8. *Letters to owners who may need to sell.* Sending out letters and postcards to sellers who may have a financial problem can be very productive. However, this process costs money and requires a good system so that you follow up on leads aggressively. I have walked into a house of a seller in foreclosure and seen a pile of letters from buyers who have written trying to buy the house. I bought the house because I knocked on the owner's door and talked with her. If you could send out 1,000 letters at a cost of $1 each and get one good lead and buy one good deal, would the letter be a good investment? Of course, but it takes effort to write a good letter and send it to the right people at the right addresses. By the way, I receive a number of letters from interested buyers—and that effort never produces a lead for them.

   You don't buy houses with letters, you generate leads.

9. *Foreclosures.* Most great deals are made because the seller has a financial problem, so a house in foreclosure seems like an obvious opportunity for an investor. However, not all properties in foreclosure are good houses in good neighborhoods. Most are not. Look for foreclosure opportunities in your neighborhoods and follow up by knocking on the door. Then it is possible that you will make some great buys.

The best deals will not have a sign in the front yard or an ad in the newspaper. The way you will find them is to walk through neighborhoods and knock on doors.

ASKING QUESTIONS TO KNOW WHAT THE OTHER PARTY WANTS

If you are calling on an ad in the paper or someone has called you, before you hop in your car to go see the house, ask the person a few questions. The answers to these questions will help you to decide which houses are potential deals and which sellers you want to meet.

If you are walking through a neighborhood and find a house that looks like an opportunity, you want to ask the owner these same questions.

In a normal market, 90 percent of the houses for sale are not opportunities. You are trying to identify that one seller in 10 who might have a reason to make you a good deal. After you find the right seller, you want to determine whether this house has the potential of making you money. Not all houses are opportunities.

Asking the right questions gives you clues about how anxious the seller is to sell the house, and then the information will help you to make an offer that the seller can accept. It will increase your chance of buying a house at a good price.

Ask these questions to determine a seller's motivation to make you a good deal. The first questions will be easy for the seller to answer. As you ask the harder questions, you are both gathering information and testing the seller's eagerness to sell. If the seller keeps answering questions, eventually the information you receive is not really in the seller's best interest to share with a potential buyer. Keep in mind that the seller is answering the questions to keep you interested in the house because he really wants to sell it.

As you ask these normal questions, take notes because you will learn a lot. Number a sheet of paper (or take notes on your computer), and record the answers.

1. *Are you the owner?* (Many times a neighbor or relative will answer the phone for an out-of-town owner. If so, ask for the owner's number and call her directly.)
2. *Where is the house?* (Only pursue houses in neighborhoods where you want to own property. Write down the address and phone number.)
3. *How large is the house?* (Look for houses large enough to accommodate a family.)
4. *How old is the house?* (Older houses may be in great neighborhoods, but beware of fragile, high-maintenance houses.)
5. *How large is the lot?* (Look for lots of normal size and shape.)
6. *Does the house need any work?* (All houses need some work. Look for an honest answer.)
7. *What school districts is the house in?* (Know which schools are the best and worst in your town. Buy in the best districts that you can afford.)

8. *What are the neighbors like?* (Are there more tenants or owners on the street?)
9. *How long have you owned the house?* (Long-term owners often have larger profits and are easier to negotiate with.)
10. *Have you made any additions or remodeled?* (Not all additions or remodeling projects add value to a house, but new plumbing, electrical service, roofs, kitchens, and bathrooms are big pluses.)
11. *Is the house listed with a Realtor?* (If so, when does the listing expire?)
12. *Do you have a current appraisal?* (If yes, ask how much it appraised for.)

These are warm-up questions. They let the seller know that you are interested and give you some basic information. If at this point you are interested in the house, move on to the following more probing questions.

Give the owner plenty of time to answer these questions:

1. *It sounds like a great house, so why are you selling?* (Listen!)
2. *Can your existing loan be assumed?* (The owner may not know, but most loans can be assumed with the lender's permission.)
3. *What is the balance on your loan now?* (This will tell you how much equity the owner has.)
4. *Are your payments current?* (Surprising enough, most owners will tell you.)
5. *What will you do if you don't sell?* (Is the owner moving anyway? When? The day before they move, most owners are really ready to make a deal.)
6. *How long has your house been on the market?* (This time. Most people answer two weeks, but it's the third time they have tried to sell.)
7. *How much did you pay for the house?* (If the owner balks at this question, tell her that you want to buy in a neighborhood that is appreciating. Ask if the house has appreciated since she bought it. In addition, you can point out that you can learn this information in the public records and would appreciate her time-saving assistance.)

8. *If you don't sell the house, would you consider renting it?* (If the owner answers this question "yes," then you may be able to buy it from him with a small down payment. He won't get much down when he rents it.)

With hundreds of possible sellers to buy from, you need to learn how to use your time wisely, and asking questions over the phone is an efficient use of your time. You will be surprised by how much sellers will tell you.

After you talk to a seller, rank both his motivation and the potential profitability of the house on a scale of 1 to 10. Below is a partial list of motivations. You will hear many other answers and can fit them into this list.

Now you can compare two or more houses directly and decide which one to pursue first.

Seller's Motivation Scale

(10 is the highest motivation)

1 The seller wants to buy a new house when she sells.
2 The seller's kids are starting school next year, and the family wants to move to another school district.
3 The seller is expecting twins and needs a bigger house.
4 The seller's in-laws are moving in, and the family needs a bigger house.
5 The seller has bought a new house, and it closes in two weeks.
6 The seller has a new job in another town starting next week.
7 The seller's wife has a new job in another town starting next week.
8 The seller is leaving town tomorrow and can't afford two payments.
9 The seller is months behind in his payments, and the sale is next week.
10 The foreclosure sale is tomorrow, and the seller will pay you to stop it.

Once you find a seller with a high motivation who owns a house that is desirable, stop looking and go buy the house!

Potential House Profitability Scale

(10 is the most desirable)

1 Older, small house in poor repair, small lot, marginal neighborhood.
2 Older right-sized house, good repair, marginal neighborhood.
3 Small house, small lot, marginal neighborhood.
4 Newer right-sized house, average-sized lot, busy street.
5 Older right-sized house, good lot, average neighborhood.
6 Newer right-sized house, good lot, average neighborhood.
7 Newer right-sized house, good lot, great neighborhood.
8 Older small house, great lot, great neighborhood.
9 Newer small house, great lot, great neighborhood.
10 Newer right-sized house, great lot, great neighborhood.

4

KNOWING HOW YOU ARE GOING TO PAY FOR A HOUSE BEFORE YOU MAKE AN OFFER

Before you make an offer to buy a house, you need to have a plan to pay for it. Your tenants can repay the money that you borrow if you pay the right price and borrow on the right terms. The first step to making a profitable deal is to figure out how much income your tenants will generate.

You do not set the rent on a house; the market sets your rent.

Some landlords try to rent their property for an amount equal to their loan payments. The tenants don't care how much your loan payments are; they will pay the least amount of rent they can for the best house they decide they can afford. Tenants will compare the houses on the market and rent the one that is the best deal.

To determine how much rent you can expect to collect, you need to study your market. Good information is available because landlords advertise their houses in your newspaper every week.

HOW MUCH CAN THE TENANTS THAT YOU WANT TO RENT TO AFFORD TO PAY?

To determine the amount of rent you can collect, conduct a rent survey of your competing landlords. Start collecting the Sunday real estate classified sections. Save them for several weeks.

Identify the neighborhoods and the price-range house that you plan to buy. Then look for houses advertised for rent in those price ranges and, if possible, in those neighborhoods.

Ads often mention both the neighborhood and the price. Circle the ads with a red pen that are in the price range and neighborhoods where you plan to buy. Call and ask the landlord who answers the phone the questions any potential renter would ask. Write down her answers.

1. Have you rented the house?
2. How big are the house and yard?
3. Is the house in good shape?
4. Is the yard fenced?
5. Is it on a busy street?
6. How much is the rent?
7. Will you accept kids and pets?
8. Is there a limit to how many people can live in the house?
9. How much is the security deposit?
10. How long must the lease be?
11. How long has the house been empty?

You will not always get an honest answer to the last question, but the reason you are calling using a three-week-old paper is that you know that if the house is still for rent, it has been advertised for at least three weeks.

You want to sort through the responses and separate the smart landlords, those who are charging a reasonable rent and security deposit, from the others who are willing to rent to anyone.

A landlord who will rent to too many people, such as six college students, can charge more than market rent. After the students move out and the landlord makes repairs to the house, he will net far less rent.

Likewise, some landlords will rent without requiring a last month's rent or reasonable security deposit. They too can charge above market rent because they will let a tenant move in who has little money. These tenants often fall behind on their rent immediately. (They don't have money!)

Surprisingly, many landlords will not answer the phone, even when they are paying a lot of money to run an ad. Some do not even have a message for a prospective tenant to listen to. When you run an ad in a newspaper to rent a house, *answer the phone*. Or if that is not possible, leave a detailed description of the house with an address so that callers can find it and then call you back if they want it.

Prepare a chart like Table 4.1, and record the information you obtain talking to the landlords. Next, go see the houses that have rented and the houses that are still for rent. Make notes about the neighborhood and the condition of the houses. Start learning about your competition. Many landlords do not buy good properties, nor do they maintain the houses well. Try to buy in better neighborhoods, and keep your houses in good condition. This will reduce your vacancies because your houses will be the first to rent.

Now you have a good idea of what your competition is, and by studying the amount of rents along with the rest of the information, you can make a good estimate of the amount of rent you can expect to collect.

RENTS AND PRICES GO UP TOGETHER AT DIFFERENT TIMES

One big benefit of investing in houses is that your rents will increase significantly over the years, whereas your loan payments can remain the same until the loan is paid off. Rents tend to increase at the same rate as prices, but in different years.

In a hot real estate market, when prices are increasing rapidly, rents will be stable and may even drop. This is a result of low interest rates that allow renters to buy houses and encourage builders to build. When interest rates are low and house prices are rising rapidly, many investors also buy houses and rent them. This increased supply of rental houses, coupled with many renters becoming homeowners, keeps rents low.

When interest rates rise, fewer renters can qualify to buy, and fewer investors buy houses for rental. These factors combine to cause a tight rental market, and rents rise as tenants compete for fewer houses.

Table 4.1 Landlord Survey

Date	Address	Phone Number	Size	Rent	Last Month's Rent	Security Deposit	Length of Stay Required	Kids/Pets (Y/N)	Has It Rented? (Y/N)	How Much
1.				$	$	$				$
2.				$	$	$				$
3.				$	$	$				$
4.				$	$	$				$
5.				$	$	$				$
6.				$	$	$				$
7.				$	$	$				$
8.				$	$	$				$
9.				$	$	$				$
10.				$	$	$				$
11.				$	$	$				$
12.				$	$	$				$
13.				$	$	$				$
14.				$	$	$				$
15.				$	$	$				$
16.				$	$	$				$
17.				$	$	$				$
18.				$	$	$				$
19.				$	$	$				$
20.				$	$	$				$

Understanding and recognizing these cycles in your town are important. Although rents will increase in the long run, these cycles often last several years at a time (see Figure 4.1).

Notice that house prices increase in some years and are flat in others. When house prices are increasing, rents are flat, and when prices are flat, rents increase. Prices typically rise during periods of low interest and easy credit. Rents increase as interest rates increase. When interest rates rise, few new units are built, and fewer tenants can qualify for a loan.

This result is more pronounced in markets prone to big swings in prices. In a market where house prices just creep up every year, it will appear that rents and prices go up together.

Although both rents and prices can experience short-term dips, in the long run they will both increase with inflation. These dips will be larger in higher-priced properties.

FIGURE 4.1 The impact of interest rates on house prices and rents

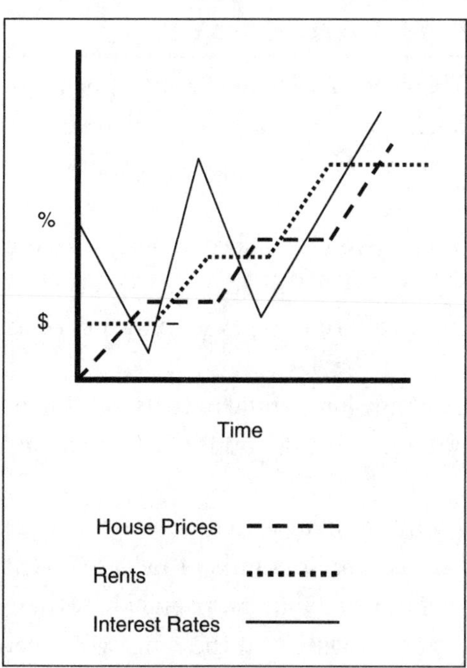

HOW MUCH WILL YOU SPEND TO OPERATE THE HOUSE?

Every house will cost a different amount to operate. Well-designed and well-built homes that have been maintained and are well situated on good lots will be far less expensive to maintain than poorly designed and built homes on troublesome lots.

You want to buy a house that will produce the most income in relation to what it will cost to operate. You might think that a very small house that would be less expensive to maintain would be best. But you want a house that is large enough to attract a good long-term tenant, and you want it in a neighborhood that will reward you with appreciation.

Use the worksheet in Figure 4.2 to project the income you will have to repay a loan.

This assumes that you will manage the property yourself. If you plan to pay a manager, plug in his fee.

HOW MUCH CAN YOU BORROW AND REPAY WITH THE RENT YOUR TENANTS PAY?

Interest rates change constantly. When you buy a house for investment, try to borrow on a long-term, fixed-interest-rate loan. Then you will be able to predict your cash flow accurately and benefit as rents increase and your loan payment stays constant.

Table 4.2 shows you the amount that you can afford to repay with the rent you collect at different interest rates. Use this chart as a guide when you are calculating how much you can afford to repay with the net rents that a property would generate.

Then calculate the exact payment any loan would have using a financial calculator. You can buy one for a nominal amount of money at any large office supply store.

Study Table 4.2 so that you become familiar with how much you can borrow to buy houses that produce certain amounts of net rent (rent after expenses). Identify the range of rents in your town, and know these numbers. Now you can make an offer knowing that the rents will cover your payments if you borrow on terms with these payments.

FIGURE 4.2 Calculating the income a house will produce

Here are actual figures for a house in my town:

Gross rent: $ 1,100 to $1,200

Using the lower end of the rent range: $1,100

	Annual	Monthly
Rent	$13,200	$1,100
Operating expenses:		
Property taxes	$1,440	$120
Casualty insurance	$300	$25
Liability insurance	$60	$5
Advertising	$300	$25
Repairs and maintenance	$1,200	$100
Total expenses	$3,300	$275
Net rent available for loan payments	$9,900	$825

ALWAYS BORROW FOR THE LONGEST AVAILABLE TERM

Using the word *always* will cause you to struggle with this idea, and this is good. Can we agree that a loan with a lower payment is a safer loan for you to owe? If you had to lower your rents to keep your house full, the longer-term loan would give you the lowest possible payment.

When you borrow to buy property, the longer-term loan allows you to borrow more money. You can buy a property with less of your cash invested.

Table 4.2 How Much Can You Repay with Different Rents?

Amount of Net Rent (Loan Payment)	Interest Rate	Loan Amount	Term
$500	6%	$83,385	30 years
	8%	$68,142	30 years
	10%	$56,975	30 years
$600	6%	$100,075	30 years
	8%	$81,770	30 years
	10%	$68,370	30 years
$700	6%	$116,754	30 years
	8%	$95,398	30 years
	10%	$79,766	30 years
$800	6%	$133,433	30 years
	8%	$109,026	30 years
	10%	$91,160	30 years
$900	6%	$150,112	30 years
	8%	$122,655	30 years
	10%	$102,556	30 years
$1,000	6%	$167,626	30 years
	8%	$137,192	30 years
	10%	$114,900	30 years
$1,250	6%	$209,531	30 years
	8%	$171,490	30 years
	10%	$143,625	30 years
$1,500	6%	$251,438	30 years
	8%	$205,788	30 years
	10%	$172,350	30 years
$2,000	6%	$335,251	30 years
	8%	$274,384	30 years
	10%	$229,800	30 years
$3,000	6%	$502,876	30 years
	8%	$411,576	30 years
	10%	$334,701	30 years

Know How You Are Going to Pay Before You Make an Offer

When you are beginning to invest, you need to use your available cash sparingly. Buying with nothing down is a better strategy than using all your cash for a down payment. If your house sits empty for two months before you rent it, you will need your cash for payments.

Even with a 30-year amortization schedule, you are paying a considerable amount of principal each month. Compare the 30-year amortizing loan with an interest-only payment (see Table 4.3).

You can pay off a loan before its due date. However, when you are still in the property-acquisition mode and can use your cash to buy a house that will make you a 20 percent or higher annual return, why would you want to use that cash to pay off a loan that is only costing you 6, 8, or 10 percent?

After you have acquired all the property that you want, you may shift gears and begin to pay off your debt. Owning free and clear real estate is a good strategy.

When you begin, focus on buying properties with long-term financing. After you own many properties with long-term loans, you can then use your

Table 4.3 Even 30 Year Loans Have Large Principal Payments

Amount of Payment	Interest Rate	Loan Amount	Term	Interest-Only Payment	Principal Payment
$500	6%	$83,385	30 years	$416.92	$83.08
	8%	$68,142	30 years	$454.28	$45.72
	10%	$56,975	30 years	$474.79	$25.20
$1,000	6%	$167,626	30 years	$838.13	$161.87
	8%	$137,192	30 years	$914.61	$85.38
	10%	$114,900	30 years	$957.50	$42.50
$2,000	6%	$335,251	30 years	$1,676.25	$323.74
	8%	$274,384	30 years	$1,829.22	$171.77
	10%	$229,800	30 years	$1,915.00	$85.00
$3,000	6%	$502,876	30 years	$2,514.38	$485.62
	8%	$411,576	30 years	$2,743.84	$256.16
	10%	$334,701	30 years	$2,789.18	$210.82

cash flow to begin reducing your debt. How long does it take to pay off a 30-year loan? About 10 minutes. You just write a check for the balance. Just because you borrow on 30-year terms does not mean that you have to wait 30 years to own your houses free and clear. Later you will learn how to pay off your debt and get your houses free and clear in far less than 30 years.

KNOWING WHAT THE HOUSE IS WORTH BEFORE YOU MAKE AN OFER

When you are buying a high-dollar item, such as a house, you need to know what it is worth *to you* before you make an offer. You cannot predict what the seller will take for the property. The amount that a property will sell for can change every day. It is the price that a real buyer and the seller can agree on on that particular day. Since both the seller's and buyer's situations can change in a heartbeat, the price that a property will sell for is unpredictable.

The property's value to you can be established. If you are trying to buy a property that produces a certain amount of cash flow or that has a good chance of appreciation in value because of its location, then you can put a price on the property that you would be willing to pay.

By researching recent sales of other properties in the immediate neighborhood that are comparable in quality and condition, you can learn what the property would sell for at a retail price. The retail price is the price that the property will sell for, given enough time (which is a long time in many markets) and exposure to the market by someone who is able to negotiate a sale. It is generally the price a competent realtor will get for a seller given enough time.

You have heard that real estate is illiquid. A more accurate statement is that it takes time to liquidate real estate at a retail price.

At a wholesale price, real estate is liquid. I will buy a house and close on it in one or two days, giving the sellers cash for their equity, at a wholesale price. This is about the same amount of time it would take the seller to sell a stock and get cash.

What is the difference between retail and wholesale? It is different with different types of real estate, so let's focus on houses. If you are buying land or commercial property, it is much more difficult to determine what a property is really worth, and the difference between retail and wholesale can be much greater.

Even with houses, the difference between retail and wholesale is different in different price ranges. The lowest-priced housing in a community generally will be in poor repair and in neighborhoods with little potential for appreciation. Lenders are not fond of making loans on such properties, and because of this, buyers are unable to obtain financing to buy these houses. This makes the lower price range less liquid, and although you can buy these houses at big discounts, when you sell them, you may have to sell at a big discount.

Some investors buy these low-priced houses because they can rent them for a high rent compared with the price they pay for the house, but these houses will require a lot of management, and the owners will not benefit from the appreciation they could with higher-priced houses.

On the other end of the price range are the most expensive houses in your town. These are more illiquid and might sell for a 20, 30, or 40 percent discount because relatively few buyers want these houses.

Anyone who can afford to buy a very expensive house has other alternatives. Such buyers can choose to buy less expensive houses, so the most expensive houses in your market also sell at a larger than normal discount if the seller is forced to sell in a hurry. This is a real opportunity for a buyer, but you must be able to afford to own the house until you can sell it at a retail price, and that could be a long time.

Houses in the middle ranges sell for closest to retail. This makes them more of a challenge to buy at wholesale prices, but it makes them safer investments in the long run. Since these houses frequently sell at retail prices, it is easier to determine their value. Research recent sales through your public records (which are often online) or through the multiple-listing service records that any realtor can provide for you.

Because these houses are more liquid, you can safely pay closer to a retail price than you could with a less liquid property, knowing that if you need to sell, you can get your money back in a reasonable period of time.

What is a wholesale price for an average house in a moderately priced neighborhood in your town? It depends on your market conditions. If there are a lot of willing buyers in your market, and lenders are willing to finance them, then a discount of 10 to 20 percent off the retail price is wholesale. It allows you to buy the house, hold it for a while, and then resell it for a profit.

There are holding costs to owning a house. An investor will rent a house as soon as possible to generate income to pay the cost of holding the house and will wait to resell until the house has appreciated. A speculator may buy a house and try to resell it immediately for a much smaller profit. Until she sells it, she must pay the holding costs, which are depleting her profits daily. Obviously, investing for the long run is a much more predictable way to make much more money with less risk.

WHEN YOU ARE BUYING, LET THE SELLER MAKE THE FIRST "OFFER"

When you are trying to get the best price, you want the other party to set his highest price first—before you make an offer. At least then you know the most you have to pay for a property. Sometimes it is a great price, and you won't have to negotiate. Typically, it is close to a retail price or even higher.

House sellers often ask for more than they expect, hoping to get lucky. Setting a price too high is not good selling strategy because it will turn off most buyers.

When you go to sell, set a price that you can defend with recent sales in your neighborhood. Document those sales and other factors, such as the cost of construction, to give your price credibility.

When you are buying a house, the price is only one of many things that you will negotiate. Some other items include the condition of the house, the personal property that will go with the house, the closing date, who will pay the closing costs, and the terms of any owner financing. You want the seller to commit on these and other issues that may come up, before you make your offer.

SCHAUB'S 10/10/10 RULE FOR BUYING GOOD DEALS

My 10/10/10 rule for buying a house states that when you buy, you make no more than a 10 percent down payment, pay no more than 10 percent interest, and buy at least 10 percent under the market. This rule of thumb will help you to put together offers to buy houses that will pay for themselves.

1. Put no more than 10 percent down. A smaller down payment is better for you in several ways.

   First, you have more liquidity. In the event that you had to resell the house quickly, it would be easier to find a buyer who can put 10 percent down than one with a larger down payment.

   Second, you have less risk because you have less to lose. The lender has more to lose when you borrow using the property as the collateral for your loan.

   Third, you can buy more houses if you use your cash sparingly.

   When you make a smaller down payment, your rate of return on your investment increases. Suppose that you put $30,000 down and buy a house that produces $2,000 a year in cash flow plus $4,000 a year in appreciation and principal paydown. Your profit, expressed as a ratio of the annual profit the property produces divided by the amount of money you have invested, is $6,000/$30,000, or 20 percent. This is your rate of return on your investment.

   If you bought the same house with $10,000 down, your cash flow would drop as your loan payment increased. Suppose that you had zero cash flow and the same $4,000 in appreciation and principal paydown. In this case, your rate of return would be $10,000/$4,000, or 40 percent. By doubling the return on your investment, you cut in half the time it will take you to reach your financial goals.
2. Pay no more than 10 percent interest on the money you borrow to finance. House interest rates vary with time—even when rates are relatively low, some investors are paying more than 10 percent to finance property.

   Since interest is the largest component of your payment, the rate of interest that you pay determines how much profit you will make on the house. Work hard to get the best possible interest rate when you borrow.

   Interest rates are changing constantly, but they are negotiable. When banks are charging more than 8 percent interest, you can still borrow at 8 percent or less from sellers and other investors.

3. Buy at least 10 percent below the market. Buying at a below-market price makes you a profit the day you buy. In addition, it reduces the amount of money that you have to borrow to buy the house, which increases your cash flow.

   It also makes the deal safer and more liquid. If you needed to sell in a hurry, you could sell to someone else at a below-market price and get your down payment back and hopefully a little profit.

Thus 10/10/10 is the worst deal you should make. You should make every attempt to buy a house with a lower down payment, borrow at a lower interest rate, or buy it further than 10 percent below the market.

If you bought a $150,000 rental house in my town today using 10/10/10, your purchase would look like this:

Market value	$150,000
Your purchase price	$135,000 (10 percent below the market)
Your down payment	$13,500 (10 percent of $135,000)
Your loan	$122,500 (30-year fixed rate at 7 percent) This rate will vary with the market
Your loan payment	$810
The monthly rent	$1,200
Monthly operating expenses	$360*
Net operating income	$840
Less loan payment	$810 (first-month principal reduction on the loan is $100.32)

*The operating expenses on a rental house will vary with the age and condition of the house, your ability to manage the property, and your local property tax and insurance rates. Buy houses in good repair that are well built, and your maintenance expenses will be significantly lower.

Calculating the net return on your down payment:

	Monthly	Annual
Cash flow	$25.00	$300.00
Loan amortization	$100.32	$1,244.36 (The first year)
Total	$125.32	$1,544.00

Net annual return on your down payment 1,544/13,500 = 11.4 percent.
Note: *This rate of return does not include appreciation.*

Do not use potential appreciation to talk yourself into buying a property. Buy one that gives you an acceptable return on your investment without appreciation, and then the appreciation will make a good deal even better.

YOUR FIRST $13,500 GROWS TO $194,000 IN A DECADE

If you hold this house until the house doubles in value ($300,000) and it takes 10 years, the loan balance would be $105,120. If you sell the house for $300,000, you would net before taxes about $194,000. If you can invest $13,500 for 10 years and receive $194,000 at the end of that time, you have earned an annual compounded rate of return of just over 30 percent. This does not include any cash flow that the property produces, nor does it account for tax benefits or costs.

This rate of return is as high as it is because of the prudent use of leverage that allowed you to buy an asset worth $150,000 with a $13,500 cash investment that then would pay for itself. It is this remarkable but *real* advantage that allows many investors to accumulate millions of dollars in net worth within a relatively short period of time.

FORMING YOUR BUYING STRATEGY

Before you make an offer, take the time to really know the neighborhood. Walk, don't ride, up and down this street and the streets on both sides of the house. Meet the neighbors. Notice what's going on in the neighborhood. Are there a lot of houses for sale or for rent? Are all the houses well maintained? Do you notice any empty houses?

Look for other opportunities. Sometimes you will find a better deal by walking and talking to others who live in the neighborhood. Ask the neighbors if they know of anyone who is selling. I wrote about this in an earlier chapter: You will be surprised at how much the neighbors know and how much they will tell you.

Research both recent sales and properties now on the market to get a good feel for prices. Rather than trying to establish an exact price for a house you are looking at, give yourself a range of prices, for example,

$140,000 to $155,000. Now, you know that if you can buy at the low end of that range or below, it's a good deal.

SET A MINIMUM ACCEPTABLE PROFIT FOR THIS HOUSE

There is some risk every time you buy a house. You will invest a considerable amount of time when you buy, rent, and sell a house. Although you are not guaranteed a profit, you should buy at a price that gives you a high probability of making a profit.

The more expensive the house you invest in, the larger your minimum profit should be. You take a smaller risk buying a less expensive house. It is easier to rent and easier to resell. You take a greater risk when you buy a more expensive house. You need to buy it further below the market to compensate you for that risk. If you had to resell it immediately, you would have to discount the price to get rid of it quickly.

Here are some examples of house prices and minimum profits. This is not a science. These numbers are to make you consider the relationship between the risks you are taking and the price you should pay for a house. You need to adjust the discount to account for the quality and location of the house and the market for houses at the time. You may decide that there is little risk in buying a higher-quality house in a strong market, especially if you can buy it with favorable financing.

House Value	Minimum Profit
$50,000–$80,000	$10,000
$80,000–$120,000	$15,000
$120,000–$150,000	$20,000
$150,000–$180,000	$25,000
$180,000–$210,000	$30,000
$210,000–$240,000	$35,000
$240,000–$270,000	$40,000
$270,000–$300,000	$45,000
$300,000+	$50,000

LOOK FOR A SELLER WHO IS TRYING HARD TO SELL YOU HIS HOUSE

Every seller and every situation are different. You want to buy from a seller who needs to sell and who is trying hard to sell you his house as opposed to someone who is playing hard to get. If you find yourself trying to convince the person to sell to you, the seller is not as motivated as you are. Look for a cooperative attitude in a seller. A seller who avoids answering questions and won't make concessions is not ready to make you a good deal.

Another test that you can give a seller is to ask her to come to you. Before I go see a house in my town, I ask the seller to come to my office for a meeting. If she won't come, she is showing me that she is not motivated enough for me to make her an offer. If she doesn't show up, I have not wasted a lot of time.

Sellers will try to get you to come see them. As a test, offer to meet the seller. If you do not have an office, offer to meet in a safe place, perhaps a bank lobby (convenient to you) or a coffee shop. If the seller does come, you will have won the first negotiation and learned something about his motivation.

There is no set formula for making offers. There is no rule that you make an offer after a certain number of hours or questions. Every seller is different. You need to test the seller to see if he is ready to sell you the property.

The way to test is to ask questions and see how the seller responds. You can ask very direct questions, such as, "Are you ready to sell your house today?" or "Can you be out by this weekend?" These questions will raise the seller's level of expectation—she will think that you are interested in buying and buying now!

You are, of course—*if* you can make a good deal.

If you ask the preceding two questions, and the seller answers yes to both, then the seller is ready for you to make an offer.

Before you sit down with a seller to make an offer, *write down your strategy*. Use the worksheet shown in Figure 4.3 to gather current market information and to think through what you want to offer. Write down the most you are willing to pay for the house, the price you hope to buy it for, and the best price you can imagine buying it for. Write down the amount and terms of the financing you need to make the house a viable investment.

It's important to write these figures down. When you are making the offer, the seller may be a better negotiator than you are and will try to talk you into paying more for the property. You need a well-thought-out plan before you actually begin the exciting process of negotiation.

Successful buyers prepare and have a game plan before they make an offer. They anticipate the seller's response and plan a counter offer. Like a chess player, a good negotiator thinks a move or two ahead. Like chess, your opponent sometimes surprises you, and when that happens, you need to step back and rethink your plan.

FIGURE 4.3 Buying strategy worksheet

House Address: ______________________________
Date: ________________

Seller's names:

____

Other houses sold in the area:

Address: ______________________________
Price: $______________ Date: ______________
Address: ______________________________
Price: $______________ Date: ______________
Address: ________________________
Price: $______________ Date: ______________

Others houses now on the market in the area:

Address: ______________________________
Price: $______________ Date: ______________
Address: ______________________________
Price: $______________ Date: ______________

FIGURE 4.3 Buying strategy worksheet (*Continued*)

Address: ____

Price: $_______________ Date: _______________

The estimated gross monthly rent the house will produce: $_____________

Estimated monthly expenses (taxes, insurance, maintenance): $_____________

Net amount available for payments: $_____________

Highest price that you are willing to pay: $_____________

Your target price: $_____________

The best price you can imagine: $_____________

The first price you will offer: $_____________

The largest down payment you can make: $_____________

The first down payment you will offer: $_____________

The amount of financing: $_____________

The terms of the financing:

Interest rate: _____% Term: _____years Payment: $_________

Your projected monthly cash flow: $_____________

Personal property and other terms or conditions important to you in this purchase:

____

____

5

MAKING THE OFFER

TALKING WITH THE SELLERS BEFORE YOU MAKE AN OFFER

After you have completed the buying strategy worksheet, sit down with the sellers and talk about what is important to them. You know what you are willing to pay. Now is the time to see if you can get an idea of *why* they are selling. The why may give you a clue as to how anxious they are to sell and how soon they need to sell.

Make sure that you are talking to the decision makers. If a husband and wife own the house, have both of them at the table. If there is another decision maker, such as a relative or an attorney, it is best to first make the deal with the sellers and then make that deal subject to review by the third party.

UNDERSTANDING THE SELLERS' MOTIVATION BEFORE YOU MAKE THE OFFER

Ask the sellers, "Why are you selling such a nice house?" Then listen.

Write down on a blank sheet of paper what reason you think you heard them say is important to them. Then show it to them to see if you heard them correctly. This may include a fast closing, a certain amount of money that they need at closing to relocate or rent another house, the relief from their current monthly payments, or money for other obligations. If they have other obligations that are bothering them (e.g., credit card bills, student tuition due, etc.), have them list them.

There are two reasons to have them list these obligations:

1. Many times they do not know exactly what they owe. One spouse may have borrowed money that the other spouse is not aware of.
2. Often you can take the responsibility for paying off an obligation as part of your purchase price. If the seller owes money to a contractor, an attorney, a hospital, or a creditor whom he is not currently paying, often you can work out a repayment plan with the creditor. Instead of paying the creditor all cash, you can pay a monthly amount, often without interest. Sometimes a creditor will agree to take less than is owed.

USING THE SELLERS' CONTRACT IF THEY HAVE ONE

Now that you know what is important to you and what is important to the sellers, the next step is to ask the sellers if they have a contract that they want to use. If they have one, use theirs. If not, use one with which you are familiar. Take your time going through it, and read it carefully when filling it out. Get the sellers to help you with it. Work together to fill out the contract.

As you fill out the contract, the sellers will need to give you information: all the owners' names as listed on the title, the legal description, and the address. Ask for the deed or title insurance policy to make sure that this information is correct.

If the sellers are cooperating, begin negotiating smaller items first, such as the personal property that goes with the house (the appliances, fans, mirrors, window treatments, etc.), the closing date, the date you can have possession of the house (if sooner), the repairs that the sellers will make before closing, and if the sellers will stay in after closing, the amount of the rent and the amount of the security deposit.

At this point you should have a good feel about how the sellers respond to your requests. If you asked for the refrigerator, and they said yes without much discussion; then you asked for the washer and dryer, and again they agreed; then you asked them to paint the bedrooms, and they agreed; and so on, you know that they are willing to make concessions to sell the house.

If the sellers refused to make any concessions that you asked for, then when you get to the more important points, such as the price and the financing, you may have to take a tougher stand when asking for things that are important to you.

DEALING WITH OWNERS WHO ARE NOT AT THE TABLE

If you are negotiating with one party in a divorce, one heir to an estate, or one partner in a partnership that is splitting up, then make your offer subject to being able to buy out the other party on terms agreeable to you. This will be a totally separate negotiation. You can pay a different price or buy on different terms. With a property that has multiple owners in title, often one will need cash today and will be willing to accept less money if he gets it now. Another owner will hold out for a higher price but be willing to accept terms.

Although these negotiations take more time, they also have more potential for profit. Of course, you need to make any purchase of a partial interest subject to being able to buy the rest of the property. A partial interest is hard to sell, and it can be expensive to force another partial owner to sell.

ASKING FOR MORE THAN YOU NEED TO MAKE THE DEAL

It is good strategy to ask for more then you really need to make the deal. The exception would be when buying from a distressed seller, which is covered later. Most sellers set the sales price a little high, anticipating that a buyer will make a lower offer. They may have a bottom-line price in mind.

Some sellers set their price way above the market, hoping to catch an unknowledgeable buyer. Don't get caught by these sellers by using their starting price as a starting point for your offer. For example, if a seller started at $200,000, don't make an offer 20 percent below his price. Even 20 percent less still may be too much.

Research what other comparable houses have sold for recently, and then compare the price of this house with those prices. Adjust the price for differences in condition or size, and then make your first offer below what you need to buy the house for to make a profit.

Suppose that a seller is asking $200,000, and after researching the neighborhood you find that other comparable houses have sold for between $170,000 and $180,000 and that they were in better shape than the seller's house. You determine that the seller's house is really worth between $160,000 and $170,000. Make your first offer far enough below the $160,000 price that you have some room to negotiate if the seller really wants to sell.

Sometimes houses are on the market for years because they are overpriced. These houses can be opportunities because eventually the seller becomes more motivated to sell, and the market values catch up with her high price.

GETTING YOUR OFFER ACCEPTED OR GETTING A COUNTEROFFER

Always try to get the sellers to accept your offer or make a counteroffer while you are sitting with them. You have already asked them if they are ready to sell their house today. If they cannot accept your offer, ask them what they will accept—*and be quiet!*

Don't let a seller who you think needs to sell simply tell you that he can't take your offer. If you let a seller leave without accepting your offer, the chances of the seller calling you back are slim to none. What will happen is that he will tell someone else what you offered, and that person will offer just a little more and buy the house.

DON'T LET A SELLER SHOP YOUR OFFER

When a seller uses your offer to solicit a higher offer from someone else, it is called *shopping your offer.* While this is good for the seller, it's no good for you. Real estate brokers who represent the seller will try to get two buyers to bid against each other to get the seller a higher price and to earn a higher commission.

You can avoid people shopping your offer by making an offer that has to be accepted or rejected in a short period of time. An offer can contain a clause that states that the seller must respond by a certain time and date, for example by "5 P.M. on July 1, 2004." If you are making an offer directly to a seller, ask her before you make the offer, "Are you ready to sell your house today?" Then make an offer. The seller needs to accept it or make a counteroffer now (or within a few hours). Never give sellers several days to think it over. They will use those days to get a higher offer from someone else.

Tell the sellers that the offer is only good today and today only. If they don't accept, your offer is off the table. If they come back to you later and want to sell, you will reconsider, but you won't guarantee to pay this much.

You can add strength to this statement by telling them about another house you are looking at and honestly saying that you cannot afford to buy them both. Tell them that you like their house better and are making them your first offer, but if they don't accept it, you will then try to buy the other house.

COUNTEROFFERS

Don't tell me what you won't do; tell me what you will do.

DEE FOUNTAIN

Dee Fountain encouraged sellers to make a counteroffer and did it with a smile so that the sellers were encouraged to make some concession to keep the deal alive. Often the offer and counteroffer process will look like this:

Original asking price:	$149,000
Your first offer:	$123,500
Seller's first counteroffer:	$145,000
Buyer's counteroffer:	$126,000
Seller's second counteroffer:	$140,000
Buyer's counteroffer:	$130,000
Final purchase price:	$134,000

The amount that the sellers move the first time indicates how eager they are to make a deal. A big price reduction like that listed above shows that the sellers are eager to sell, and this is a sign to you, the buyer, to make small increases in your offer.

Another good question to ask sellers is, "Would you buy this house today for what I am offering you?" If they turn down your offer, they have, in effect, just bought their house for that amount—they could have had your money instead of their house.

NEVER GIVE A SELLER A BIG DEPOSIT

When you make an offer, you typically show that you are serious by including a deposit with the contract. Do not give the seller this deposit. Make your check out to an attorney or title company who will handle the closing.

If you need to gain creditability with the sellers by showing them that you have the money necessary to buy their house, you could bring a cashier's check payable to your attorney or title company with you and attach it to your offer.

This check does not need to be for the full down payment. A check for $1,000 should be enough to show that you are serious.

Often if you are agreeing to close within a short period of time—a week or two—agree to make the deposit with the attorney or title company within 48 hours after they have accepted your offer. If you are signing a contract on a weekend, you typically have to wait until Monday morning before you can give the attorney or title company your check.

This gives you time to raise the down payment if you don't have it and a way out of the deal if you change your mind. The language in your offer will determine who gets the earnest money and what happens with it in the event that either the buyer or the seller fails to close.

Use language that protects you. The contract may state that you are entitled to a refund of your deposit if you don't close because of certain reasons; for instance, an inability to finance the property. It may state that the sellers can keep your deposit if you don't close, but that is all that they can have and that you have no other liability in the deal. The language in a broker's contract is more likely to favor the seller and the broker over the potential buyer.

If a real estate agent is involved, the agent will want to hold the deposit. Give the agent the smallest amount possible. One hundred dollars is sufficient if you are agreeing to close in a week or two. Both the seller and the broker will want more deposit money if the closing date is months away.

LOOPHOLES

When you make a written offer that can be enforced by the other party, always give yourself a way out of the deal. This way out is commonly called a *loophole* or a *contingency.* It should be simple and clearly understood by both parties. Two common reasons that a buyer may choose not to close are

1. An inability to borrow the money to buy the property
2. Undisclosed defects in the property discovered during inspection

A contract can contain a clause that allows the seller to cancel the contract and walk away without further liability for either or both of these reasons. If the contract calls for a short-term closing, typically these clauses are acceptable to a seller. If your offer calls for a long-term closing and still gives you the right to cancel the contract up to the date of closing, a knowledgeable seller would object and want to limit the contingencies to a shorter period of time. More on loopholes will be offered in Chapter 7.

HOW TO USE A HOME INSPECTOR AS A SAFETY NET

Hiring a home inspector to give a potential purchase a good look is a great idea. The home inspection business is relatively new, and I have done my own inspections for years. I always called in one of my repair people if I thought we had a problem with a roof or plumbing and so on.

Now you can hire a home inspector for a few hundred dollars who will check out all the major systems, such as plumbing, electrical, heat/air conditioning, and the structure and roof. Not all inspectors are equally good at what they do. Meet them at the house, and walk around with them. Don't pester them with too many questions, but watch them work and learn from watching. You will learn a few tricks that you can use yourself.

They will give you a written report that you then can use to negotiate further with the seller in the event that you find a previously undisclosed problem with the house. If you have already negotiated a great deal, don't be foolish and ask for more if the problems you discover are small. Your counteroffer will let them out of the obligation to sell to you, and they may then sell to another buyer for more money.

Instead, use the home inspection as an insurance policy against major problems that you otherwise might miss. If you are having second thoughts about buying the house after reading the inspection, this means that you have not made a great deal and that you should ask for more concessions from the seller. You are then willing to risk the deal getting away; you are asking for more, not out of greed, but to make the deal safer for you.

HOW TO HANDLE A SELLER WHO WANTS A THIRD PARTY TO APPROVE A CONTRACT

Sometimes a seller will want her attorney or a family member to look over or approve a contract. Often this is done because the seller does not understand the contract. Try to make your offers as simple as possible.

If the seller insists on having a third party involved, use language that keeps the deal together, unless the third party can introduce new information that influences the seller's decision. For example, with an attorney, insert a clause that says, "This transaction will close as agreed unless Attorney __________ [enter the attorney's name] notifies both the buyer and seller in writing within three days stating how the contract is not in compliance with current statutes and regulations."

Never say that it is "subject to the approval" of an attorney or anyone else. No attorney would ever put his stamp of approval on anything that might subject him to liability.

Likewise, if Uncle Harry has loaned the sellers money and wants to give some advice with his money, state that "this transaction will close as agreed unless Uncle Harry notifies both the buyer and the seller in writing within three days stating how the transaction is not in compliance with current statutes and regulations."

FOUR SECRETS TO GETTING YOUR OFFER ACCEPTED

Buyers are more likely to accept an offer that they understand, that gives them instant or near-instant gratification, and that requires them to do little work.

First, keep your offer simple. Avoid long, complicated contracts. Sellers will refuse to sign them simply because they can't understand them.

Sellers need to know how much money they are going to get and when they are going to get it. Be as specific and clear as possible on these two points.

Second, make a net offer with you paying all the closing costs. Know what your closing costs will be, and calculate them into your offer. This gives the seller the answer to "How much money will I get?"

Third, offer to buy the house in "as is" condition. This allows the seller to leave the house without doing any work. By taking all the risk, you can increase your profit. Of course, you need either to inspect the house thoroughly before you make the offer or to make the inspection a contingency in your contract. Even with this type of offer, you can require the seller to leave the house in its current condition, without further damage. Walk through the house before you close to make sure that it is in the same condition as it was when you inspected it. If there has been additional damage, you can renegotiate the price to compensate for it.

Finally, offer to close quickly. Often sellers will accept lower offers that close sooner. They are selling because they need money now. If they could wait, they could sell for more.

If you can incorporate all these items in your offers, you will buy houses further below the market and buy more houses.

Figure 5.1 is a checklist that will take you step by step through the process of finding, negotiating, and closing your first deal. Use it for every house you buy.

FIGURE 5.1 Buying and closing checklist.

1. Identify a potential bargain purchase; ask questions.
2. Write down the one urgent problem you can solve for the seller.
3. Establish the fair market value, give or take 5 percent.
4. Research the market rent and likely net income the property will produce.
5. State your minimum acceptable profit on this house.
6. Formulate an offer that solves the seller's one urgent problem.
7. Make the offer. Insist on either an acceptance or a counteroffer (*Don't tell me what you won't do; tell me what you will do*).
8. Make another offer based on any new information.
9. If the seller is unresponsive but you remain convinced there is opportunity, go away and come back in a week with another offer.
10. Get the contract accepted—signed by all parties.
11. Make your earnest money deposit with the closing agent.
12. Retain rights to house inspector and termite inspector if needed.
13. Order a title search with a title company, attorney, or escrow company, and furnish these agents a copy of your fully signed contract.
14. Talk with the agent or attorney who will prepare the closing documents to alert him to any unusual clauses in the contract.
15. Get copies of any documents you will be required to sign the day before the closing, and get a copy of the title insurance commitment—read to check for exceptions.
16. Read closing documents (very carefully!!!).
17. Walk through the house the day of the closing after the sellers are completely out of the house.
18. Go to the closing, review the documents, and collect the appropriate items listed on the closing documents list, and get the keys and garage door opener.

Note: When you are buying, take your time. Time is on your side. Having both the buyers and the sellers at the closing can work to your advantage. When you are selling, sign documents in advance. Only go to pick up your check after the buyer has signed everything and left.

Source: Reprinted from John Schaub, "Making It Big on Little Deals," seminar by permission of Pro Serve Corporation of Sarasota, Inc.

6

BORROWING TO INCREASE YOUR PROFITS

When buying real estate, you can increase your profits significantly by using leverage. Most real estate investors who are millionaires today, started with only a little money. They bought their first property with a small down payment, at times using none of their own money, and then they bought another property as soon as they could. They continued to buy, one property at a time, getting better terms and prices as they learned more.

The secret to being able to buy property that will make you rich is to learn how to borrow on terms that your tenants can repay with their monthly rent. Buying a property with little or nothing down is a great strategy, as long as you can afford to make the payments. If you can't afford to make the payments, you will never collect any profits.

YOU CAN BORROW A LOT WITHOUT TAKING A LOT OF RISK

When you borrow to buy real estate that produces enough income to repay its own debt, you can sleep well. Whether the property goes up or down in value, the lender will not call you for more money. As long as you can afford to make the payments, you can ride out a recession, and wait for the houses to go up in price before you sell. Recessions tend to be much shorter in duration than the periods of economic prosperity that follow them. Look at recessions as buying opportunities.

Lenders prefer houses as security for their loans over other investments. The proof of this is that they are willing to lend a higher percentage of the purchase price to the buyer of a house than to the buyers of other types of investments. The interest rates on house loans are often the lowest because the risk is the lowest.

The reasons for this favorable treatment are the stability and long-term history of appreciation of the housing market. Houses may not go up every year, but they go up almost every year. Every town is different, so national housing statistics may not apply to your town or your houses. The national market is influenced by interest rates and the availability of credit. If it is easy to borrow, more people will buy. If it is easy and cheap (low interest rates), then people will buy as much as they can.

Economists describe the supply of houses as "inelastic" because it can take years to develop lots and build new houses. The demand for housing easily can outrun the supply. When you have many buyers competing for a limited number of houses, they bid the prices up. The opposite happens when there are a lot of houses and not many buyers. They bid the prices down.

This inelastic nature of the supply of houses makes it difficult for builders and developers. They may be halfway through a five-year project when the demand drops. Then they must reduce prices to sell their product. Look for opportunities to buy new houses at discounted prices when builders overbuild in a rising-interest-rate market.

As you gain experience, you will buy more of your houses when there is an oversupply (a buyer's market) and sell when there is more demand than supply (a seller's market). You never want to be forced to sell in a buyer's market.

When you borrow money to buy property, always borrow for a long enough time to allow you to wait for a seller's market to sell. Interest rates typically will be lower in a seller's market, so it is also the time to "harvest," or refinance, your good houses that you want to keep indefinitely.

BORROWING A MILLION DOLLARS AND STILL SLEEPING WELL

Do you think that you will ever owe a million dollars? If you buy ten $100,000 houses, you could easily owe $1 million. In some markets, investors are buying million-dollar houses for rental investments. If they buy with leverage, they can owe a million dollars on one house.

The key to sleeping well while you are in debt is knowing that you can repay the debt. When you buy rental houses, your tenants will repay your debt if you buy and finance wisely.

My friend, Jack Miller, says that the surest way to become a millionaire with real estate is to borrow a million dollars, buy property, and then pay it off. Even if the property never appreciated, you would have your million dollars.

Jack is right. If you will learn how to borrow that million dollars safely so you can sleep well, then you are on your way to unlimited financial success. The safety comes from borrowing against property that generates enough income to repay the loan.

Most people can't conceive of borrowing that much money. This is so because they are thinking about going to the bank and qualifying for a million-dollar loan. You can borrow from sources other than banks without qualifying for a loan based on your income and credit.

BUYING HOUSES WITHOUT BORROWING FROM BANKS

As I wrote earlier, when I started investing in houses, I was a self-employed real estate salesman with no track record of making money. Not one banker in my town would loan me money to buy property. As it turned out, that was a key to my success. It forced me to learn how to buy property without going to a bank to borrow money.

There are many sources of borrowing other than going to your banker. Borrowing from a bank takes longer and costs more than other sources. When you borrow from your banker, she will charge you the current retail rate of interest and in addition charge for anything else she can to increase the bank's profits. The paperwork the bank uses will protect it, and if you read the fine print, it is not good for you. Yet nearly everyone borrows from banks.

If you have a good job and good credit, banks will loan you money for a few house purchases, but borrowing from banks is never cheap. If you buy a lot of houses, you will find that all lenders have limits to the amount of loans that they will make you, and eventually, the banks will refuse to make you more loans.

THINGS YOUR BANKER WON'T DO

Bankers have a lot of rules to follow. The rules are both imposed by the government and self-imposed by the banking industry. Before a banker lends you money on real estate, he will want an appraisal, a credit report, proof of your income, and a list of other debts and assets that you have. If you start buying property aggressively, you will soon reach the point where the bank rules will limit the number of loans you can have with one lender. These rules make borrowing from banks both time-consuming and agonizing.

1. *The first thing a banker won't do is loan money to someone who really needs it.* If you need it, then you must be in trouble or almost in trouble, and bankers hate trouble.

   If you know you are going to need money one day, borrow before you need it. You may really need it because you are about to be temporarily unemployed, or divorced, or unable to pay your taxes. Whatever the reason, it will be hard to borrow when you are in trouble.
2. *Your banker won't loan you 100 percent of the purchase price of an investment property.* If your goal is to buy a property with nothing down, then you will have to find a lender other than a bank. Some sellers will sell you a property with nothing down. Typically, they are sick—either sick of managing or sick of making payments. Look for burned-out investors who have bought several properties but never learned to manage. They often will sell to you with a low down payment and carry all the financing to get out of management. Even a small payment is more money than they can get when they rent to a tenant.

Some borrowers try to trick bankers into lending them more by using fake contracts or phony appraisals. This is called *bank fraud,* and you will go to jail if they catch you. Typically, the lender does not go to jail, just the borrower who provided false statements.

Beware of those who tell you to lie or use devious methods to buy or borrow. Understand that many lenders work on commission and that they are under pressure to lend money. If you are uncomfortable with what they are asking you to do, get a second opinion from another lender or an attorney.

3. *Your banker won't make a decision fast enough to loan you the money to buy a really good deal.* What is a really good deal? It is when a seller has decided to sell today at a bargain price. It is typically a time problem. The seller is out of time and needs money today (or very soon) or something (generally something bad) is going to happen.

   I have purchased several homes from sellers the day before their house would be sold at a foreclosure auction. Although they may have had chances to sell before, they waited until the last minute to make a decision. At that point, there were few buyers willing to take the risk of buying on such short notice and able to close in one day.

   Even though I have great credit and can qualify for a loan today, there is no banker in my town who can close a real estate loan the same day I call him for the money. Later we will discuss the use of home equity loans and lines of credit. If you have these available to you, they can be used for quick purchases at bargain prices.

4. *Your banker won't make you a loan if monthly payments are not made or if the first payment is due in a year or two.* In fact, bankers typically insist on monthly payments starting right away. This is a problem if you are buying a house that will sit empty for a while.

   Other lenders are willing to lend on terms that allow you to make repairs without making payments.

THINGS A SELLER WILL DO THAT YOUR BANKER WON'T DO

When a banker loans you money, she writes you a check. She is going to be very cautious and charge you a high rate of interest because she has borrowed the money she is lending to you from her depositors. She has to pay them back, so she can't take big chances with their money.

When you buy a house from a seller who wants to get rid of it, the seller is not lending you money, he is waiting for his equity or profit from his house. This may be equity or profit that he will not get if he does not sell to you.

He is not as cautious as the banker lending money. He just needs to be comfortable that you will make his payments and eventually pay him.

Consider the following purchase:

Selling price:	$150,000
Market value:	$165,000–$175,000
Seller's purchase price 20 years earlier:	$40,000
Potential bank loan (80% of purchase price):	$120,000
Actual seller financing:	$140,000

With this house, the seller had a large profit because he had owned the house for 20 years. Most sellers have profits, and many are willing to carry a note and take their profit over several years.

A banker making a $120,000 loan has no profit until you begin making payments. What looks like a risky deal to a banker can look very safe to the seller of a property.

BORROWING CREATIVELY–ON TERMS THAT YOUR TENANTS CAN AFFORD TO REPAY

A wonderful feature of investing in property is that you can structure the financing on a property so that your tenants make all the payments. The key is to borrow on terms that have payments that your tenants can afford to make.

Sometimes this requires a combination of financing on different terms. For example, suppose that you can buy a house worth $200,000 for $180,000. The gross rents are $1,600 a month, and the net income after taxes, insurance, and repairs is about $1,100 a month.

If you borrowed the entire $180,000, what interest rate and term would you need to have payments low enough that your tenants would repay the loan?

To answer this question, you need either an amortization schedule or a financial calculator, which you can purchase at any large office supply house for a small amount of money. If you don't have a financial calculator, get one. Learn how to calculate both payments for different loan amounts, terms and interest rates, and the rate of return on your investment. Then you will be able to compare two potential investments.

With a financial calculator, you can solve for one variable if you know the other three. In the preceding question, what interest rate can I pay and how much time would it take to repay the $180,000 purchase price with $1,100 a month in net income?

I know the amount ($180,000) and the payment ($1,100). To find an answer to the interest rate or term, I need to plug in one of the variables.

Amount of Loan	Interest Rate	Term	Payment
$180,000	?	30 years (360 months)	$1,100
The solution is 6.18 %.			

Now suppose that you have to pay 7 percent today for money; you could solve for the term you would need. If you know that you can borrow at 7 percent for 30 years, then you could solve for how much can you borrow:

Amount of Loan	Interest Rate	Term	Payment
?	7%	360	$1,100
The result is $165,338			

What if you cannot borrow enough money at today's rate to buy the house and repay it with the cash flow the tenants will produce? Then you need to borrow part of the purchase price at a lower rate, or with lower payments, or with deferred payments.

Suppose that you need to borrow a total of $180,000, and you find a source that will lend you $150,000 at 7 percent for 30 years.

Amount of Loan	Interest Rate	Term	Payment
$150,000	7%	360	$997.95

After making the $997.95 payment, you have $102.05 a month (this year—your rent should increase with time) to use to pay the other $30,000. Each year your cash flow should increase as rents increase.

Here are four ways to repay $30,000 with $100 a month:

1. Pay the seller (or a friendly lender such as your parents) $100 a month without interest (300 months).
2. Pay the seller $100 a month beginning when you can raise the rent enough to start making that payment.
3. Pay the seller $100 a month now and agree to increase it as you increase the rents. You can take your best guess at rent increases and design a repayment schedule based on your projections: say, $100 a month year one, $125 a month years two and three, $150 a month years four and five, and so on.
4. Pay the seller the whole amount ($30,000) in one lump sum 10 years from now. This may cause you to either refinance or sell at that time unless you have saved the money to make the payment.

BUYING EMPTY HOUSES WITH ZERO-INTEREST SINGLE-PAYMENT NOTES

Owners with an empty house will finance the amount of their equity with no payments for a while if you will begin making the payments on their existing bank loan. These sellers have a big problem; they own an empty house that may cost them $1,000 a month or more every month. Few people have an extra $1,000 a month in their budget that they can use to make payments on an empty house.

I have purchased many houses by agreeing to start making payments on an existing loan and agreeing to pay the sellers the amount of their equity, without payments or interest, when I sold their house. This could take years, but in the meantime, they have no more big payments to make.

You may be asking how you will be able to make the big payments that the seller can't make. The answer is that you will rent the house to a tenant who will pay you enough to make the payments. Before you make an offer on any property, know how much it will rent for and what your operating expenses will be so that you know how large of a payment you can make.

Suppose that a seller owns this house:

Their purchase price:	$80,000
Today's market value:	$160,000
Their existing loan:	$120,000
Their equity:	$40,000

Offer the seller a note for $40,000 with no interest and no payments until you sell the house or in seven years if the house has not sold. You agree to begin making the payment on the existing $120,000 loan. Secure this note with a second-position mortgage or deed of trust on the house. In the event that you cannot make the payments, you can deed the house back to the seller.

The major benefit to the seller is that she gets immediate relief from both the payments and the responsibility of maintaining the house. If the seller wants to buy another house, she can show the new lender the agreement with you in which you took responsibility for making the payments on the first loan.

You get to buy a house with nothing down that will produce enough income when rented to make the payments on the first loan. When the house appreciates enough that you can refinance it or sell it at an acceptable profit, you will have the cash to pay off the second loan to the seller.

AVOIDING HIGH-RISK TRANSACTIONS WHEN BORROWING FROM SELLERS

Beware of schemes to borrow money in ways that put others at risk. For example, if you buy a house from a seller who agrees to let you put a new first mortgage on the property and then pay the seller part of his equity secured by a second loan on the property, you easily could borrow more than the property can repay. If you cannot make the payments and the house falls into foreclosure, the seller will lose his equity.

For example, a house is for sale for $200,000. The buyer offers to pay the seller $100,000 at closing and to give him a second mortgage for the other $100,000, subject to borrowing $150,000 against the house with a new first mortgage. The buyer then puts a new first mortgage against the property for $150,000. After the closing, the buyer has $50,000 in cash less his expenses and owns a $200,000 house with $250,000 in debt against it. Generating enough income to repay $250,000 in debt will be a real challenge.

If the buyer uses the cash he received from the new loan to make the payments, it will run out eventually. If there is a foreclosure, the seller with the second mortgage likely will realize a large loss.

Some would call this fraud, but it is probably fraud, only if you intentionally structure a deal with the intent of not repaying the loan. If someone made this deal over and over again and did not pay the sellers their equity, it may be fraud, but in any case, it is bad strategy.

Borrowing your profits before you earn them is not sound business strategy. It's like taking an expensive vacation you can't afford and paying for it with a credit card. The result is often disastrous, both for the buyer and for the seller.

USING INVESTORS TO FUND YOUR DOWN PAYMENTS

When I started buying property in my early twenties, no banker in town would loan me a dime. I quickly learned that there were other investors willing to put up down payments for property if I would do the work of finding and managing a property.

Suppose that you need $30,000 for a down payment. Think about people you already know who like real estate and believe that it is a good investment but do not want to be involved with the hands-on activities of buying, managing, and selling.

Most people do not invest in real estate because they don't want to deal with the tenants, nor do they want to negotiate the purchase and sale of a house. They don't know how to make a good deal or manage tenants, and they won't take the time to learn.

Many have money in the bank and recognize that real estate is a good investment. *Never get involved with someone who has to borrow the money to invest*. Look for an investor who has money in the bank or in a securities account earning little. They need you, and you can use their money to make them much more than they can earn in a bank or in the stock market.

The are several advantages to using an investor's cash for the down payment:

1. It does not have to be repaid until you sell the property.
2. You make no payments on it and pay no interest until you sell the property.
3. Using an investor's cash to make a larger down payment and close quickly, you can negotiate a bigger discount on the price.
4. Using the investor's cash for a larger down payment will reduce the debt on the property and increase the cash flow, making the house a safer investment.

STRUCTURING AN AGREEMENT THAT'S GOOD FOR BOTH SIDES

To give the investor a better return than he can earn with a bank account or most other passive investments, you can agree that instead of borrowing the $30,000 and paying interest on the money, you will split the profits that the house makes. Profit produced by buying the property below the market and appreciation will be taxed at the lower capital gains rate. The investor also may be able to shelter some of his current income from taxes with the depreciation the house produces.

For your part, you will agree to find and buy the property, manage the property, and then—years from now—handle the sale. The investor's part is to put up the down payment and, if necessary, qualify for and sign the loan. When you borrow using an investor, limit your loan to 75 percent of the value of the house, and your rents will cover the payments. It will be a low-risk loan and should be an easy loan for any investor with good credit to obtain.

Your plan is to hold the house until it doubles in value, and then sell and split the profits with the investor 50/50, after repaying the $30,000 down payment he made.

Today's market value:	$200,000–$220,000
Your purchase price:	$180,000
New loan:	$150,000
Down payment from investor:	$30,000

You hold the house until it doubles in value.

Sales price when it doubles:	$400,000
Approximate loan balance:	$140,000 (this amount probably will be lower)
Gross sales proceeds:	$260,000
Repay the down payment:	$30,000
Balance of sales proceeds:	$230,000
Your 50 percent:	$115,000
Investor's 50 percent:	$115,000

You made $115,000 with no money invested, but you used your time and skill to find a good deal, buy it, and manage the property and the tenants. The investor made $115,000 profit on his $30,000 investment, without ever talking to a seller, tenant, or a buyer.

These numbers are just round figures to make it easy to understand the concept. With a real house, you and the investor would have income during the holding period. This income can be split 50/50, or you could take all the income and give the investor a larger share of the profits. Talk with your certified public accountant (CPA) about the concept of using a limited liability company (LLC) to hold title and to allocate income and expenses.

OWNING PROPERTY WITH AN INVESTOR

There are several ways to hold title to a house with an investor. You want to protect both parties' interests and use easy-to-understand documents and agreements.

The best way to protect your interest is to be named on the title to the property. The best way to document your agreement to manage the property is with a short and clear management agreement. Because you are also an owner of the property, you would not need a real estate license to manage the property (a nonowner may need a license to manage investment real estate in some states).

HOLDING TITLE AS TENANTS IN COMMON

A simple way for investors to own a house together is to have the investor buy the house, finance it, and then deed to you an undivided one-half interest with the loan in place. All these papers can be signed at one time at the closing of the property and recorded in the proper order in the public records. You then would be an undivided one-half owner on the public records, holding title as tenants in common.

This is not a partnership, and *you should not call it a partnership*, nor file a partnership tax return. Each owner actually owns an undivided half of the house. Each owns half the roof, half the lot, and so on.

Because you actually own one-half of a house, you could sell your half interest to another person, but few buyers are interested in buying half a house. The plan is to hold the whole house until you sell both halves to a new owner.

If something unexpected happens to your investor—he dies, he loses a lawsuit, or he files bankruptcy—then his half may be transferred to a new owner, but you would still own your half. An advantage of holding title as tenants in common is that claims against the investor's half will not attach to the other half that you own.

All that is required to hold title as tenants in common is the proper language in the deed. You can go into title and borrow the money together to acquire the house. Or, as suggested earlier, the investor can go into title, borrow the money, and then deed one-half interest to you. If you buy and borrow together, then you will have to furnish financial statements and pay for credit reports and other expenses.

HOLDING TITLE IN A TRUST, CORPORATION, OR LLC

Another way to hold title that has the advantage of keeping the names of the owners off the public records is to form a trust, corporation, or limited-liability company (LLC) or limited-liability partnership (LLP) to own the property. These entities either can pass through the income and expenses to the owners or pay the taxes before making distributions. An advantage of using an entity that can be taxed as a partnership is that you can make disproportionate distributions of income and allocations of expenses.

These entities require documentation and may be required to file an annual tax return. To be used wisely, they require a good understanding of how they work.

One disadvantage is that lenders often will not lend money on properties that are owned by trusts or other entities. The bankers may require you to hold the title personally to finance or refinance. Some states require you to use an attorney to evict tenants owned by corporations or LLCs. Insuring properties held in different entities may be a challenge. If using these entities to hold title sounds more complicated and expensive, it is.

When you are dealing with other people's money, you want to be cautious, and you want to be sure that documents are prepared, executed, and recorded or filed properly. If you want to form a separate entity to hold title, find a competent attorney with lots of experience in forming these entities. There are advantages and disadvantages to taking title in a separate entity. Obtain both legal and tax advice before spending thousands of dollars to form and maintain an entity that you may not need.

BORROWING FROM OTHER INVESTORS

Many people have money in self-directed retirement accounts or other accounts that they will need in the short run and are not willing to invest in property. They may be willing to invest in a relatively short-term loan that would pay them more interest than they could earn in their bank account.

Bankers have high overhead and pay depositors a small fraction of what they charge their borrowers. If you cut out the middleman, the bank, you can borrow directly from depositors and pay them far more than the bank will. It can still be an affordable source of down payment funds for you.

An additional advantage of borrowing from a private source is that you sometimes can negotiate a loan with no payments due until you sell the property. If your lender is a pension plan that is not going to distribute the income to the beneficiaries for 10 more years, the fund doesn't need the money back soon. The fund can make you a three-year loan with interest to accrue that you could use to buy a property and repay it with interest when you sell.

The biggest concern of private lenders is getting their money back. They are not as concerned about earning a high rate of interest as they are in getting their money back. Try to oversecure any money that you borrow from a private lender. Give private lenders more than one property if you need to so that they will feel secure. A secure lender is a happy lender who sleeps well, and such a lender will lend to you at a reasonable rate of interest.

Avoid the lenders who charge 16 to 24 percent plus points, plus prepayment penalties. Only a speculator who is buying and selling a property in a short time can afford these rates. The speculator is giving the lender a share of the profit and has to pay the high rate because he is often borrowing 100 percent of the purchase price.

USING HOME EQUITY LOANS AND LINES OF CREDIT

There are several advantages to these commonly used loans. A line of credit is an unsecured bank loan that you can obtain based on your credit and ability to repay it. You borrow only what you need when you need it and typically pay interest only on the balance until you repay the loan. These interest-only payments are lower than payments required on an amortizing loan.

The disadvantage of lines of credit is that there may be a requirement to pay the loan off within a certain period of time. Another disadvantage is that the interest rate typically is tied to the *prime rate,* the rate set by the big banks. This rate can change with time, and your payments can increase.

A good customer with great credit may be able to negotiate a rate at prime or even below prime. Most borrowers pay 1 or 2 percent above the prime rate.

A home equity loan is a line of credit that is secured by your personal home. Because it is secured, there is less risk to the lender, and the interest rate is often lower than you can negotiate on an unsecured line of credit. Again, you typically can arrange to pay interest only on the outstanding balance, although the interest rate will change with time.

These loans are useful for buying a house that you plan on selling for a short-term profit or selling to an investor to recover your investment and keeping half interest. They are not advisable for a house you want to hold for many years because the rates and your payments could increase dramatically.

If you borrow using your home equity line at 6 percent and rates jump, you could soon be paying 12 percent interest, or twice your original payment. If you borrowed to buy a house and the rents just covered your payments, with a higher interest rate the rents would not cover the payments.

If you cannot repay a home equity loan, you could lose your home.

Use this money carefully. Only use it to buy bargains that you know you can sell for a short-term profit or to an investor so that you can repay this loan before interest rates change dramatically. Know that when interest rates are rising rapidly, it may be harder to sell a property quickly for a profit.

REFINANCING A HOUSE YOU OWN TO BUY ANOTHER HOUSE

If you are committed to buying several houses, your strategy for buying and financing them is important to your long-term success. Just buying houses won't make you rich.

New investors often assume that the best way to get the down payment for a second house is to refinance the first house. Logically, they would then refinance the second house for the down payment on the third house and continue to refinance to pull out cash for new investments.

Refinancing is a good strategy to reduce your interest costs when rates drop, and you can increase your cash flow. When you refinance and pull cash out of a property, you are increasing your debt, and often you will reduce your cash flow.

Consider the result of refinancing this house to get the down payment to buy another house:

Appraised value of house:	$180,000
Percentage a bank will loan to investor:	80 percent
Amount of new loan:	$144,000
Estimated closing costs (3 percent):	$4,320
Payoff on old loan:	$100,000
Net cash available for down payments	$39,680

REFINANCING DOES NOT MAKE YOU RICHER

Note that before you refinanced this house you had $80,000 in equity, the difference between the value of the property and the loan balance. After you refinance, you would have $36,000 in equity and $39,680 in cash for a total of $75,680. Your net worth has dropped by the amount of the refinancing cost.

Refinancing is not a profitable move unless you reduce your interest cost significantly so that the interest you save repays your cost of refinancing in five years or less. If you sell the house in less than five years, you will not even recover your refinancing costs. Lenders know that many loans are either paid off or refinanced in five years or less, so refinancing is a profitable business for them.

The other risk of refinancing is that despite your intentions to buy another investment property with the proceeds, those new cars and exotic vacations are very tempting. Either have the house you want to buy under contract so that you know where you will spend the refinancing proceeds, or put the funds in a separate account (not your personal checking account). If the money's in your personal account, you may yield to temptation and spend some or all of it on toys or good times.

An alternative strategy may be to put a second mortgage on this investment house and avoid paying the closing costs on the $100,000 balance on the old loan that you get no benefit from paying off. Second mortgages often have higher interest rates. Compare the increased interest cost to the closing costs you can save by not refinancing the whole amount.

Closing costs when borrowing typically include a credit report, an appraisal, title insurance on the new loan, recording fees and state taxes, sometimes points (interest paid in advance), and miscellaneous fees that the lender tacks on. These costs often equal about 3 percent of the new loan amount.

Whenever you borrow, recognize that some of these costs are the same regardless of how much you borrow. If you only borrowed $124,000 in the preceding example, netting you $20,000, but had to pay closing costs on the whole amount, your costs would be a much higher percentage of the money you borrowed (4,320/20,000 = 21.6%, 4,320/39,680 = 10.88%).

INCREASING YOUR PROFIT DRAMATICALLY WITH A PHONE CALL

Always ask for a discount when paying off any loan. This may seem strange to you, but lenders, especially private lenders and some smaller banks, want their money back sooner. To get it sooner, they will take less than the full face value—but only if you ask them to do so.

You must make this offer before they know that they will be paid off. You can ask them this way, "I was planning to pay off some of my loans, and yours was one I was considering. Would you be interested in being paid off today rather than over the next 10 (use the real remaining loan balance) years? If so, my closing costs to refinance and pay you off would be $4,320. Would you be willing to pay that amount if I paid your loan off now?"

You receive discounts by asking for them. I owed one seller $10,000 due in less than one year. She accepted a $4,000 discount to get her money nine months early. It would have been smarter for her to wait the nine months. Where else could she earn $4,000 on a $6,000 investment in nine months? Of course, I knew that I was going to pay them, but some lenders never know that they are going to get paid until the check is cashed. The certainty of money today, rather than waiting for it, is worth a lot.

Check with your tax advisor on how to report any discount you are able to negotiate. The amount of the discount probably will be taxable, but if you save $4,000 and owe a tax of $1,000, you are still $3,000 ahead.

BEING EFFICIENT USING A REFINANCING STRATEGY

Interest rates and the credit market have cycles. When the rates are low and credit is loose, borrowing money to restructure your existing debt or to finance new purchases can be profitable. When interest rates are high, you don't want to replace a low-interest loan with a high-interest loan to get money for a down payment.

If you are a long-term investor, you can play the cycles. When rates are low, borrow what you will need not for just one house but for several purchases. It costs less to refinance one house than three houses. If you can, refinance just one with the most equity to get the cash you need for the down payments for the next several houses.

7

UNDERSTANDING AND USING REAL ESTATE CONTRACTS

Real estate contracts can be confusing and even intimidating. Many agreements are several pages long; most have been prepared by attorneys and contain language that can be difficult to understand.

With preparation, you can understand any contract and use contracts to your advantage. The key is to take the time to read and understand any contract before you are under pressure during a negotiation.

You need a written contract to buy, sell, or rent a house for several reasons.

- To be enforceable, a contract that deals with real estate must be in writing. The Statute of Frauds recognizes that real estate agreements often involve large amounts of money and can be complicated. By requiring that a contract be in writing to be enforceable, it reduces the number of misunderstandings and litigation. You can buy a house without a written contract. You cannot force someone to perform, however, if he changes his mind.

- You want everyone to have a clear understanding of the deal, and you want the contract to cover as many issues that might arise in the negotiation as possible. Whether you are buying or selling, the contract is the guideline for the person who will prepare the documents needed to close, such as the deed, closing statements, and any note, mortgage, or trust deed.
- You want to give yourself a graceful way out of the transaction in case you discover something that makes this a bad deal for you. This may be what is commonly referred to as a loophole in the contract.
- The contract can help you in your negotiations.

USE THE RIGHT CONTRACT

Only sign a contract that you have had time to read carefully and fully understand. You may spend dozens of hours finding and researching a good deal, and if you buy it, you will spend hundreds of more hours managing and eventually selling it.

Take an hour or two, or whatever time you need, to read any contract carefully before you sign it. Many people sign documents that they do not fully understand. They may discover later that they have made concessions worth thousands of dollars unknowingly because they signed a contract they did not understand.

Attorneys often will prepare a contract from standard clauses, which they have on a word processor. Most agents and many laypeople use a preprinted form contract. Typically, a joint committee of attorneys and agents gets together and approves these preprinted form contracts, which then become the commonly used contracts for residential purchases in their state. Other contracts are available at office supply stores.

If you are presented with a contract that an attorney drafted, read it especially carefully, and question any word or phrase that you do not understand. If an attorney prepared it, she probably was working for the other party, and the conditions in the contract will reflect the other party's perspective.

Take your time asking questions; you are not paying the attorney's bill. If you're using your attorney, get him to fax you a copy before you intend to sign it so that you can take your time and read it carefully. Attorneys occasionally use confusing or unclear wording. Make them say it in English. One attorney prepared a document so convoluted that he could not explain it to me. It was back to the drawing board for him, without pay.

It is important to use a form that is designed for the type of transaction you are making. A contract designed for residential sales would have inspection and financing clauses that you would not find in a contract used to buy and sell land. Read the form carefully. You need to understand how it affects you and to make sure that it is the right form for the job.

FORM CONTRACTS PROTECT THE SELLER, REALTOR, AND ATTORNEY

Remember that a Realtor almost always represents the seller and that a committee of agents and attorneys typically designs these contracts. These form contracts are designed to legally bind both parties but often have clauses that give the seller and Realtor, as well as the attorney, more protection than the buyer.

As a buyer, you need to understand what you are signing and read carefully any form contract ahead of time. Get a copy of a contract (a Realtor with whom you might do business would be a good source), and practice by filling in all the blanks as if you actually were purchasing a house. Read all the fine print to see what it requires you to do and what happens if you do not perform.

Beware: There is no "standard" contract. Even these form contracts often are modified to give one party an advantage.

Sometimes sellers will have a contract, and it can be to your advantage to use their contract. Read it carefully, looking for unusual provisions that favor the sellers. Take your time, and if possible, take a copy of the contract with you so that you can read it word for word. If you are ready to make the offer now, go over the contract with the sellers, asking them questions about anything that is unclear to you.

IMPORTANT BIG-MONEY CLAUSES YOU NEED TO UNDERSTAND

Several key clauses in a contract are critical to your financial welfare. Read the whole contract, but read these clauses especially carefully. You will look at these clauses differently depending on whether you are buying or selling.

Inspection Clause

A buyer typically is given the right to inspect the property that he is purchasing. This right of inspection may last only a few days, or it could last right up to the closing date. The remedy available to the seller, if the buyer finds something wrong with the property, is the key to this clause.

If the buyer simply can walk away and recover his full deposit, then the seller is left with no money and no leverage to make the buyer perform. If you are the buyer, this is great. The clause may require the seller to fix items that cost up to a certain percentage of the purchase price. You can be sure that the buyer always will find something wrong with the property. There are no perfect houses.

If you are the seller, you want the buyer to approve the property within a short period of time *or* to provide you in writing a list of the deficiencies in the property. As the seller, you may want the right to fix the deficiencies and close the deal or the right to cancel the contract. Another option would be that the buyer receives a certain amount of credit and is required to close the deal.

Regardless of what the contact says, you can negotiate a settlement when a problem is found. If you are selling, it is better simply to give the buyer a credit and to let him make the repairs. This gets the house closed faster and puts the burden of making the repair on the buyer. If the seller makes the repair, it is not rare for the buyer to complain about the quality of the repair work. Don't put yourself in this position.

If you are the buyer, then you may want the seller to make the repairs, which gives you more time before you close. If you are borrowing money to buy the house, the lender may insist that the repairs are done before it makes the loan.

Just before closing (typically on the day of the closing, within hours of the time the papers are signed), the buyer inspects the house one more time. This is commonly called a *walk-through inspection,* and the purpose is to ensure that the house is in the condition promised in the contract.

Again, this inspection is better for the buyer than for the seller. If the seller has not made agreed-on repairs or has not left the house empty and clean, then the buyer has several choices. First, the buyer can refuse to close until the house is put in good condition. Second, he can insist on holding back part of the seller's proceeds until the house is clean and in good repair. Or third, he can renegotiate the price of the house.

Often the seller just wants to get the deal closed and is willing to renegotiate the price. Knowing this, if this situation comes up when you are buying, be prepared to ask for a lower price that reflects the cost of the needed repairs or cleaning.

Closing Costs

By custom, and sometimes by law, buyers pay certain closing costs, and sellers pay certain closing costs. Sometimes a lender, such as the Veterans Administration (VA) or the Federal Housing Administration (FHA), will require that a seller pay the buyer's closing costs. Generally, you can negotiate who will pay these costs, and they can be substantial.

First, learn if your state requires a seller or buyer to pay a certain cost, for instance, the tax to record the deed or note. Next, learn which costs customarily are paid by the buyer and which costs are paid by the seller, such as title insurance, appraisals, loan closing fees, and so on. Although many of these fees typically are paid by the buyer, they still may be negotiable.

Just as a buyer can ask for a credit for repairs that need to be made, the buyer also can ask for a credit toward the closing costs of a new loan.

Paying a higher price and getting a credit for the closing costs may allow a buyer to borrow a higher percentage of the purchase price.

Assuming or Taking Subject to Existing Loans and Liens

When you purchase a property that has an existing loan or existing liens recorded against it, you have three choices:

1. You can pay off those loans and liens.
2. You can assume the obligations and agree to pay them.

3. You can buy the house, paying the seller for her equity, and take title to the property *subject to* the loans or liens on the property.

If you agree to assume a loan, you are agreeing to become responsible for repaying the amount owed on the loan. The lender typically will require that you apply for a loan assumption and charge you for that privilege. There is often a fee, and when you assume the loan, it will show up on your credit record.

If there are liens to other creditors, you can agree to pay them off at closing or assume the responsibility to pay them. If you agree to pay them off, then the seller may hold you to that agreement, and if you do not pay them, the seller may sue you to force you to pay the creditor. Be careful what you agree to when assuming a loan or a lien. Read the language in the contract carefully, and modify it, if necessary, to protect yourself.

When you take *subject to* rather than assuming a loan, you are not agreeing to pay these loans or liens, you are simply acknowledging that there is a loan or a lien against the property. Your contract should state clearly that you are buying subject to the loans, and the sellers should understand what this means. The loan will still be in their names.

Because the loan is in their name, it may affect their ability to borrow money. If they are facing foreclosure, they are far better off if you begin making the payments rather than letting the loan go through foreclosure. When you begin making on-time payments on the loan, it will actually improve their credit. Most sellers who will sell to you subject to a loan are in financial distress and cannot make their payments. The lender is also in better shape when you begin making payments. The lender normally would rather have the payments than the property.

Of course, if you buy a property and take title subject to a loan and then are unable to make the payments, you will lose your down payment and any other money you invest in the property. But—and this is an important *but*—you have no legal or ethical responsibility to pay such a loan. If you decide to walk away from this property because you cannot make any money with it, you can walk with a clear conscience.

Don't buy a property unless you are confident that you will make money. In 33 years of buying properties and taking title subject to existing loans, I have made money on every deal, and in every case I made the payments.

The typical reason to take title subject to existing loans and liens is when the seller owes more on the property than you are willing to assume. You want to avoid the personal responsibility for repayment.

Some properties are burdened with high-risk debt, debt with a high interest rate, or a short-term loan that requires high payments. You do not want to guarantee to make payments on this high-risk debt. If you cannot make the payments, you want the option to give the property back to the seller or to the lender without any further responsibility.

In the last recession, several builders gave me the equity in their new houses, and I agreed to take them subject to their debt and begin making payments to the lender. The builders were unable to make the payments and faced foreclosure and potential bankruptcy. The lenders were delighted to begin receiving payments.

I had to scramble to find good tenants during a recession.

While bankruptcy is more common now than in the past, many people are proud of their good credit record. They will do all they can to avoid a foreclosure or a bankruptcy.

Discounting Existing Liens

If you choose to pay off the liens when you buy a house, you may be able to negotiate a discount. I bought a house from a couple who had a bank loan, another loan to the builder that they had bought the house from, and a third lien on the house owed to an attorney for an unpaid legal bill. In talking with the sellers, I learned that the builder had promised to make repairs and had never made them and that the attorney had never completed the work.

I agreed to buy the house and make the payments on the bank loan but not formally assume it. I further agreed to pay off both the builder's lien and the attorney's lien if they gave me permission to negotiate with both the builder and the attorney. Next, I contacted both the builder and the attorney and offered to pay them that week if they would accept less money. Both agreed to a substantial (more than half) discount and were happy to receive the money. I was able to buy the house at a significant discount because of the discount the lien holders agreed to take.

Specific Performance

A specific performance clause requires one party (or both parties) to fulfill the contract. It is more likely that the seller would be required to sell the property (by a judge, if necessary) than a buyer would be forced to buy the house. But either or both parties can be held to the exact terms of the contract if there is a specific performance clause. When you are the buyer, you want to be able to walk away from a contract, with the right to forfeit your deposit. Being able to walk away gives you a way out of a deal. You may find a better deal or discover something about this property that you really don't like, or your world may change.

ALL YOU NEED IS ONE GOOD LOOPHOLE

We talked about making loopholes briefly in Chapter 5. A *loophole* is a way out of a contract. You don't need a dozen ways out of a contract, just one good one. In all my years of buying, I have never used a loophole to get out of a deal. The secret is to make your offer good enough that you don't want out.

Sometimes small problems arise, or you discover something unexpected and expensive that's needed to fix the house. A loophole is not designed to protect you from these little things. A loophole protects you if big problems arise in the deal or with you personally. It's like a major medical policy. With small issues, though, remember that every house has little things wrong with it—they are part of the reason you are buying at a good price.

If you discover that the house you are buying has a foundation problem that would be very expensive to correct, you will want a way to get out of the deal. Likewise, if you had a serious financial setback or maybe an accident that would make closing problematic, you will want a way out of the deal.

A good, commonly accepted loophole is an inspection clause that allows you to unilaterally cancel the contract up to the closing date. Every house has something wrong with it. Most inspection clauses give the seller the right to correct the problem and close or to cancel the contract. You want a clause that obligates the seller to close but allows you to cancel the contract without giving a specific reason that then could be debated or corrected.

The clause could read, "The buyer has the right, at his expense, to inspect the house or to have the house inspected by a contractor or inspector; in the event that the buyer is not satisfied with the results, the buyer has the right to terminate this contract without further liability." Have your attorney review and approve this clause before you use it.

When you buy a house at a good price, typically the seller is in a hurry to sell, and the reason you were able to get the good price is that you have agreed to close quickly. Most of my closings take place in less than a week after I sign a contract. A clause that ties up a property for months would not be acceptable to many sellers. They would be taking their house off the market, and you would have the right to cancel the contract right up to the closing.

THE AMOUNT OF YOUR DOWN PAYMENT

When you are buying with a relatively quick closing, two weeks or less, then you can make a nominal deposit, say, $100, with your offer. Recently, agents have solicited offers from me asking for no down payment. Sellers and brokers will want more money down if you want a longer time to close. If there is an agent involved, he may have an agreement that allows him to keep half of any deposit you forfeit if you don't close.

It is obviously in your best interest not to make a large deposit. In the rare event that you would want out of the contract, you would have less to argue about.

The only reason to make a large down payment is to convince the seller that you are a serious buyer. You can get the seller's attention with less money by making an offer that closes in a week.

PICKING THE PRICE FOR YOUR OFFER

The sellers should have given you the price that they are trying to get for their property. When you are buying a house, you should be making your offers at a low enough price or with such good terms that you will be happy if the seller accepts. If you make an offer that the seller accepts and then you feel bad, you have offered too much.

Plan ahead to make your offer good for you. Don't be overly concerned about what the sellers will accept. They will let you know if you are too low.

AFTER YOU SIGN THE CONTRACT

After you and the sellers sign the contract, make a copy for each party. If you have no way to make a copy, make two originals. Have the other party fill out a duplicate original by hand, proofread it carefully, and everyone sign both copies. You keep the one they filled out. It would be hard for them to claim that they did not understand the contract if they actually filled it out.

CONTRACTS CAN BE MODIFIED

If you need to change any provision of a printed or typed contract, you can by striking through the part that you want to change and writing the change near the part you struck through. If the change requires lengthy language, then using a separate addendum would be advisable.

Make any changes clearly, striking through the number or conflicting language in the printed contract. Have all parties to the contract initial any changes, and if you use an addendum, have all parties sign and date it.

USING A REALTOR'S CONTRACT WHEN BUYING THROUGH AN AGENT

Typically, when you are buying a property through an agent, the agent will want to use his contract. It will protect the agent and generally offers the seller, whom the agent represents, more protection than the buyer.

You can modify this contract to please you or use a separate addendum if you need to make changes or additions that won't fit on the contract. Often these Realtor contracts have a lot of fine print and little space to make additions or changes, so an addendum is a good way to add what you need to make the offer acceptable to you. Remember to strike through any words or phrases or complete sections that your addendum supersedes.

ADDENDUMS

Use a separate written addendum when many or lengthy modifications are required. If you use an addendum, have all parties (including the Realtor) sign and date it. The addendum should refer to the contract it is modifying. For example, "This is an addendum to the contract between Joe and Sally Seller and Bob and Betty Buyer, dated January 5, 2004, regarding the property described as 123 Paradise Way, Sarasota, Florida."

You could add a complete legal description, but the address is sufficient because you will then attach the addendum to the full contract, which has a legal description.

Your addendum could include your inspection clause. It also may contain a clause dealing with existing loans and liens that you may want to keep on the property rather than pay them off at the closing.

USING AN INFORMAL AGREEMENT

Although you need to be careful in writing down your first few deals, professional buyers often use an informal agreement before actually filling out a binding contract. In Donald Trump's book, *The Art of the Deal,* he explains how he typically negotiates all the important parts of a deal without using a contract and then gives his notes to his attorneys to incorporate in a binding agreement.

The only contract I had for one of the largest transactions I was involved in was a large brown envelope on which the seller and I diagrammed a deal including 13 properties and several financing transactions. It closed without a hitch because we both wanted to close and were able to work out the details that we had overlooked using the envelope.

Often when I am buying a house I will outline my offer one step at a time on a yellow pad or blank sheet of paper so that the sellers can both hear me and see in simple terms how I am willing to buy their house. Most sellers have little experience in buying or selling property. You cannot go too slowly or make it too simple when explaining an offer.

Sellers have two big questions they want answered:

1. How much will they be paid?
2. When will they be paid?

NEVER GO TO COURT TO ENFORCE A CONTRACT

Sometimes sellers will change their mind and refuse to close. Your contract may give you the right to force them to close. Don't do it.

It is easier and more profitable to find another good deal than it is to force a seller to comply with a contract. To go to court will cost you thousands of dollars in attorney's fees and take many hours of your time. In the end you would get to buy the house from a seller who may be mad at you. It is far less aggravation and better business simply to walk away from this deal and look for another one.

If the seller has found another buyer who is willing to pay him more, ask the seller for part of the profit. It is better for the seller to pay you part of the profit than to go to court to resolve the problem.

If you willingly agree to cancel the contract rather than fight to keep them in the deal, sellers sometimes will change their mind. One seller called me to cancel a deal, and I told her I'd be glad to because I had found another house I liked better. Then she reconsidered and wanted me to close.

8

SECRETS OF PROFESSIONAL NEGOTIATORS

You are a negotiator—we all are. Some are better than others because they have learned from their experience how others react to certain offers. You can level the playing field with these good negotiators by recognizing their techniques and being prepared for any negotiation that involves a lot of money.

A penny saved is a penny earned.

BEN FRANKLIN

I suspect that Ben Franklin was an excellent negotiator. He understood that saving a penny when you buy something is the equivalent of earning that same penny—and that was before we had an income tax.

Today, when you save a penny or $10,000 because you buy something at a below-market price, you have saved even more than the discount you made. To pay the extra dollar to buy something, you first have to earn that dollar plus the tax you owe on it. Saving $1,000 when you buy something is the equivalent of earning the $1,000 plus tax.

Donald Trump uses this technique to make millions of dollars tax-free. He bought a house in Palm Beach, Florida, for more than $1 million below the market. His million-dollar profit is tax-free to him and always will be tax-free until he chooses to sell the house.

Real estate investors understand this concept and use their skills to buy properties at large discounts that are tax-free to the buyers unless they decide to sell.

Several of my students use this idea to reduce the amount of tax they pay while at the same time increasing their yearly "earnings." These high-income individuals choose to reduce the number of hours they work at their normal professions. This reduces their taxable earned income.

They then spend those hours buying property at bargain prices. They may earn $100,000 working "part time" and then buy several properties at a discount of even more than $100,000 during the hours that they spend as buyers. The discount they earn is untaxed until they sell the property, if ever.

LEARNING TO BECOME A GOOD BUT FAIR NEGOTIATOR

If you are going to buy, sell, and manage real estate, then you need to learn to negotiate. As you become good at it, you will make a lot more money. Negotiation is probably the most valuable skill that you can acquire.

> *Negotiating has a bad reputation. It is not the art of taking advantage of someone else. It is the art of putting a deal together.*

Some sellers never sell because they have no skills in getting a buyer to commit to buy, even when it would be very good for the buyer. Landlords have vacant houses because they never get potential tenants to commit to renting.

Negotiating is a skill you can acquire, although many people seem to be born with it. Take a three-year-old to a store and you will experience how a persistent negotiator, who won't take no for an answer, can get what he wants.

There are several secrets that successful negotiators use to reach an agreement. Notice I did not say to *win,* but to reach an agreement. Unless both parties to a negotiation receive some benefit, even if they agree in writing, the deal generally will fall apart, with one party failing to perform as agreed.

ONE-SIDED DEALS OFTEN FALL APART BEFORE CLOSING

An example of a failed negotiation is when a salesperson uses an emotional argument to get a buyer to sign a contract. Such a close might be that this house is offered way below the market value and that another buyer is on his way over to sign a contract. If you want to buy it, you need to make an offer right now, or it will be gone.

After a contract is signed under this kind of pressure, the buyer may check out other houses for sale and learn that the house that he bought was not a bargain. He would then do what he could to get out of the contract, using excuses such as a lack of financing or deficiencies in the property for not buying.

Another example is a buyer who drives a hard bargain with a builder and negotiates such a good price that the builder cannot build the house at a profit. The builder may then cut corners during the construction, delivering an inferior house, or simply refuse to build the house.

Some people would be quick to hire an attorney to enforce their rights under a one-sided contract. The argument is that once everyone agreed, then every party should be forced to comply. Hiring an attorney and going to court to enforce a contract, however, is rarely a profitable adventure.

If you find that you have negotiated a one-sided deal and determine that the other party cannot perform reasonably, then reopen the negotiations. See if you can negotiate a deal that will work. If you consider the cost of both sides hiring an attorney and going to court, it is far cheaper to give a few dollars on each side to make the deal work. In addition, going to court will delay you and take a lot of your time. The total cost makes suing someone to enforce a contract that was one-sided to begin with an expensive misadventure.

There are many approaches you can take to a negotiation. Figure 8.1 presents four examples of results that are somewhat predictable depending on the approach that you take.

Here are outcomes for each of these types of negotiations:

I Win/You Lose

You are buying from a seller who is short on time and resources and must sell. You make the seller a low "take it or leave it" offer. The seller takes it but goes away mad.

Another example may be when you are dealing with another professional negotiator, such as a lawyer, a banker, or a Realtor. You know you have the advantage and use it to make a profit. "It's not personal, just business," as they said in *The Godfather.* An example may be when you find a property in foreclosure and recognize that a bank will lose a significant amount of money unless it makes a deal today. You make the bank a low offer, which it accepts for a small loss but recovers most of the money it loaned.

You Lose/I Lose

When one party in the negotiation has most of the power, typically the party with the money, then that party can overleverage the other party by making an offer that so offends the other party that he won't take it or continue negotiations. A "take it or leave it" low offer to a homeowner who is behind in his payments is an example.

You Win/I Lose

Sometimes it is wise to lose a negotiation. I recently had a long-term tenant call me to ask if I would pay for half the cost of the paint if he would

FIGURE 8.1 Negotiation matrix.

I Win / You Lose	You Lose / I Lose
You Win / I Lose	I Win / You Win

provide the labor to repaint the interior of several rooms. I said no, that I would not pay for half the paint—I would pay for it all if the tenant would use my favorite color, antique white.

I often "lose" negotiations with good customers that I could easily win because by losing I enhance our long-term relationship, and that relationship is often very profitable.

I Win/You Win

When a seller is under a lot of pressure to sell, you make her an offer that allows you to make a reasonable profit but leaves her enough money to move and rent another home to live in, and you also give her the time to move.

QUESTIONS TO ASK BEFORE YOU NEGOTIATE

1. *Is the person with whom I am negotiating able to make a binding decision?* If not, ask who can make that final decision and negotiate with that person.

With smaller transactions, such as a purchase at a store or when borrowing money at a bank or buying a car, you typically are dealing with an employee, not an owner. The owner would have authority to negotiate and make a binding decision. An employee may have some negotiating authority but typically will seek approval before making a commitment.

When borrowing from a bank, the banker who interviews you when you apply for a loan may give you the indication that he will make you the loan, but typically he will need the approval of the loan committee, which may be a committee of one, the boss. Bankers typically have a certain *loan authority,* the amount that they are authorized to lend without further approval. The higher you move up in the bank hierarchy, the larger the loan authority, until at some level a real committee would approve the transaction.

When you are buying or selling a house, you are often dealing with a married couple or sometimes two partners who own a house together. The decision to buy or sell is typically a joint decision, and you need to involve both parties in the negotiation because they both will have to sign the contract.

2. *Is it worth my time to negotiate?* Although some people consider it fun to negotiate for everything, rather than trying to talk a store clerk into giving you a discount on a loaf of bread, save your energy for the purchase where you can save several dollars or several hundreds or thousands of dollars.

> *Once you reach fifty, you should not have to negotiate for everything.*
>
> JIMMY BUFFET, *A PIRATE TURNS FIFTY*

Most day-to-day negotiations involve little potential to make a profit. Plan ahead to be well prepared for the bigger negotiations that are worth hundreds or thousands of dollars to you. By being prepared for the big negotiations, you will profit considerably, allowing you to follow Jimmy Buffet's advice.

3. *How will this negotiation affect my relationship with this person/company, and are future negotiations with this person/company likely to be important?*

Many negotiations lead to another negotiation. The first interaction sets the stage for the second. Those with whom you negotiate can be a source of referrals—or result in lost business. If you aim to be a long-term success in your business, then positive referrals can be a large part of your business.

When you rent to a tenant, the tenant has the potential to be a source of income to you for a long time. The tenant also may refer other friends to you or steer others away from you. How you negotiate with this tenant will affect how she treats your house and what she tells others about you as a landlord.

Many of my tenants have been referred to me by other tenants. This is not because I am a pushover but because I deliver a good house at a fair price, and I'm predictable in how I respond to tenant requests. McDonald's has built a billion-dollar business not because its food is the cheapest or even the most tasty but because its food is predictable. You know what you are going to get. I have built my tenant management business using the same principle. Fair and predictable. No surprises. It works.

4. *Is this the best time and place to negotiate?*

Timing

When you are the buyer, you get to choose when and where to negotiate the purchase. You want to be well prepared and in good shape both physically and mentally before you begin negotiation.

Have a good meal, be well rested, and take plenty of time to think through what you plan to say. Only when you are at your best and well prepared should you negotiate for tens of thousands of dollars.

You want to have a plan. If things are not going according to your plan, you take a break and regroup. When you are the buyer, you are in control of the situation. Walking away and then starting again can work in your favor as the buyer. The seller will see you as a serious buyer when you come back, and you can pick up the negotiation where you left off last time.

Although I close some properties within a week, I often take weeks and occasionally months to buy other properties. I visit with the owners a number of times, and each occasion moves me a little closer toward my goal.

WHERE TO NEGOTIATE

When you are buying a family's home, it is better to negotiate the purchase somewhere other than in the home—for many reasons. The first reason is distractions. Their home is full of distractions from kids and pets to perhaps the neighbors dropping by.

If you are going to make an offer in their home, you need to take charge of the situation and eliminate as many distractions as possible. One of my students is a very successful buyer and often buys sitting at the seller's kitchen table. To eliminate distractions, he first pulls the "for sale" sign out of the yard and puts it alongside the house. Once inside, he takes charge of the situation by turning off the TV and taking the phone off the hook. He wants to reduce the distractions while he is buying the house. If the sellers object to this, he knows that they don't want to sell to him that day.

I prefer to ask the sellers to meet me outside their home. I ask them to bring their file on the home, including their purchase documents, current insurance and tax bills, and a current loan statement. This is asking a lot of these possible sellers, and it is a test.

If the sellers are only mildly interested in selling, then they will decline my offer. If they really want to sell, they will meet me with all their information. Because I am a wholesale buyer, I only want to meet with sellers who are ready to sell and need to sell now.

Look for an office you might have access to because of other business that you do, such as a conference room at a bank or title or escrow company. This more professional setting has advantages over a coffee shop, such as copy machines, but a coffee shop can work. When I teach classes on buying property, my students actually find sellers and make them offers. Many of those offers have been made in coffee shops or 24-hour restaurants, and hundreds of successful negotiations are concluded there.

BEFORE YOU NEGOTIATE

Secrets of Professional Negotiators

Know the value before you make an offer. Based on the rental survey you conducted, you will know how much rent the prospective tenants will pay and therefore how much you can afford to borrow and repay if you buy this house. You also will have tracked comparable houses that have sold and be able to establish a price range within a range of 10 percent.

1. *Negotiate for the things that are least important to you first.* You may begin by negotiating for the appliances. If the sellers won't agree to include the appliances, you may adjust your strategy to continue to ask for several minor items, such as making repairs to the house or a delayed closing date. It's okay to lose on these issues, but wait to negotiate the issues that are more important to you last. At that point, you have reached agreement on many issues, and the sellers will have a lot of time and emotion invested in selling you their house. You can use the momentum created because you have made concessions to conclude the negotiation at a price and on terms acceptable to you.
2. *Invoke the doctrine of fairness.* One of the best negotiators I know is my friend Jim Napier. One of his favorite negotiating techniques is to raise the issue of fairness when it appears that one

party is taking unfair advantage of the situation. An example might be when one party continues to prevail on every issue. After one side wins on several issues, it only seems fair that the other side should win something.

By negotiating with a plan, you can strategically lose many issues that are less important to you, holding out for the one item that is critical to you in the negotiation. It might be the price, the down payment, or the terms of the sale.

After you spend considerable time negotiating seriously with the sellers, they become confident that you will buy their house. After you have reached agreement on many points, then is the time to negotiate the point or points most important to you. Now you can invoke the doctrine of fairness, if necessary, reciting all the concessions that you have made to try to put this deal together.

3. *Never bid against yourself.* I once sold a house at an auction. There were only a few serious bidders, and one bidder got so excited about buying the house that he bid twice in a row. He bid $65,000, and when no one else acted, he made another bid of $70,000. He raised his own bid, bidding against himself.

   You may think that this seems funny, but during actual negotiations for a major purchase such as a house, it is very exciting—and it is easy to raise your own bid. It generally happens when the other party just does not respond to your offer.

   Silence can be a powerful tool. If you offer the sellers a price for their house and they simply don't respond, what is your reaction? Typically, it is to offer more. A seller who understands this can get you to bid against yourself.

   I once bought a property from Jim Napier. I made him an offer, and he just looked at me. He said nothing, but I thought his look conveyed that he did not think that the offer was good enough. After what seemed like a long time, I asked him what he thought would be a fair price. He still did not respond, so eventually I offered him a little more, trying to get him to engage in negotiation. His silence eventually forced me to bid against myself. It's a powerful tool, but it takes some practice before you actually can use it effectively.

4. *How to negotiate with an agent.* The best deals I have ever made have been brought to me by agents. In Chapter 9 you will learn how to negotiate with and through an agent.
5. *When there are two or more sellers and they are hostile to each other.* When there is a divorce or another partnership that is breaking up on less-than-friendly terms, you need to negotiate with the parties separately. Sometimes, when an estate is settled, several heirs will end up with a property. They may not even know each other, but it is almost certain that they will have different needs and demands. One may need cash right away and will sell quickly to get it, whereas another will want a higher price and be willing to wait for it.

   This can become an advantage to a buyer when handled carefully. Anything you say to one party may be communicated to another party, so you want to take the high ground and never disparage the other parties, even though the person you are with may have a lot of ugly things to say.

   Your job when dealing with multiple sellers is to find out what each one needs and when and then to structure an offer to buy just the one share on those terms. Then approach the other, or another, heir as noted in the preceding section on multiple owners.

   A twenty-something heir may want quick cash to buy a new car or take a vacation. You could agree to buy his share at a wholesale price and close quickly. An older heir may want a higher price but be willing to accept payment for her share over a number of years to supplement her retirement income. A third heir may want to occupy the property for a time or even keep an interest in the property, thinking that it will be worth substantially more in a few years. You can make a separate deal with all three.
6. *Getting on the same team with the other party.* Have you ever made an offer to buy a car from a dealer and have the salesman leave you to get approval of his sales manager? What happened? Typically, the salesman returns with the bad news that he could not give you that much for your car or that he could not sell the car for that little, and then he will try to talk you out of more of your money.

He blames the other party (in this case his manager) for the higher price and tries to befriend you. He will work hard for you to try to get you the best deal he can.

Notice this technique because it is one of the best negotiating strategies. Rather than set up an adversarial relationship with the buyer (you), the salesman puts his arm around you (figuratively, if not literally) and becomes your ally in this battle against the sales manager.

Together, as a team, you will come up with a strategy that the sales manager will accept. The salesman will become your knight in shinning armor and do battle with the enemy until you finally prevail.

In the end, the salesman will congratulate you on being a tough negotiator and then congratulate you on making a great deal. You will go away thinking that you really made a good deal and feel good about your purchase. That is the way a successful negotiation should end.

You don't have to worry about the car dealer going out of business. They are professionals, and before they started talking with you, they knew the lowest offer that they would take for the car you bought. Their process is geared to getting you to pay more than their lowest number.

I took my teenage son with me the last time I bought a car and told him what was going to happen at each step of the negotiation. He was pretty impressed that I knew almost exactly what the salesman would say and what techniques he would use.

Buying a car is actually pretty predictable. The salespeople have done it hundreds of times and know what works and what doesn't. The next time you buy a car, pay attention to the salesman's technique, and rather than playing the role he expects, have a little fun. On a slow day, it can be fun and good practice to drop by a dealership and negotiate to buy a car even if you don't really want to buy one. If it's a slow day at the dealership, the salespeople will be happy for a little practice themselves, and if they are good, they may make you a deal you can't refuse. Be careful unless you want a new car.

The next time you go to buy a car, do something unexpected, and see how the salesperson reacts. After the salesperson comes back with the bad news from the sales manager, rather than increase your bid, ask to use the phone and call somebody. Call a competing car salesperson whose card you brought with you and explain the deal. I guarantee you that that salesperson will promise you a better deal.

Now give your car salesperson one more chance to reduce the price rather than increasing yours. Be nice. Tell the salesperson that you would rather do business with him because you do like his car and his dealership better. Turn the tables on him, and get him to bid against himself.

If he tells you that he can't do any better, thank him for his time and stand up and start to walk out. Before you hit the door, he will ask you to give him one more chance to get his manager to meet your price. If he thinks that you are ready to buy that day, he won't let you leave without doing his best to make a deal.

If you are in the business of buying or selling something and you have a real customer who wants to do business with you, you don't want that customer to walk away without making a deal. Buyers or sellers who walk away often make a deal with someone else. When you find yourself with a seller who needs to sell or a buyer or prospective tenant who likes your property, work hard to make the deal now. If they leave to think it over, you rarely will see them again.

7. *Know when to walk away.* Some sellers are in so much trouble that you may not be able to buy their property even though they desperately need to sell. One seller had several young children, and her spouse had walked out on her. She was months behind in her payments and desperate for some cash to move into a rental property. The lenders would not cooperate, so she had no equity in her house, and there was no profit potential for an investor.

   In cases like this it is tempting to pay the seller too much for her house, just to help her out. What this seller needs is charity, not for you to pay too much for her house. If you truly want to help, write her a check for moving expenses, but don't buy her house for too much money. Try not to confuse business with charity. Make money in your business operation, and then be generous with your charitable gifts. There are a lot of people who need your help.

NEGOTIATIONS AND NEGOTIATORS TO AVOID

Not everyone plays by the same rules. Some people will do anything to win a negotiation, including lying and outright stealing. It is foolish to think that you can outsmart these people or that you can keep them honest even with a great contract.

Avoid negotiating with people you find to be dishonest. Even if they agree to a deal, they will not honor their agreement. They will either refuse to close, or they will start negotiating all over again.

The great majority of people are honest, and once they have reached an agreement, they will perform as they agreed. If you find yourself dealing with a dishonest person, walk away. It will save you both time and money.

WHEN A DEAL IS GOOD ENOUGH, QUIT NEGOTIATING AND BUY

One of the best buyers in the country is Jack Miller, who says it this way: "Don't steal in slow motion." A good buyer knows when to quit talking and get the contract signed.

If a seller is ready to make you a great deal on his property, stop negotiating! Don't ask for anything more; just accept his offer. To do this, you need to be ready to buy. You need to know what the property is worth, know how to fill out a contract, and know how you will pay for the property.

The best deals happen quickly. Selling and buying a house are as much emotional decisions as business decisions. The day the sellers decide to get rid of the house and move on, they will make some buyer a good deal. If you happen to be in the right place at the right time, that could be you, if you have the ability to make the deal right then.

9

BUYING AND SELLING WITH AGENTS

Some of your best buys will be through licensed real estate agents. There is a misconception that agents buy all the good listings. It's not true. In fact, any informed agent knows that it is a conflict of interest to buy his own listing. An agent does not represent his client's best interest by buying that client's property at a bargain price.

I use the term *agent* rather than *Realtor* because the term *Realtor* is a registered trademark of the National Association of Realtors and refers only to its members. While only some agents are Realtors, all Realtors are agents.

TRAINING AGENTS TO CALL YOU WITH GOOD DEALS

How can you convince agents to call you when they find a good deal? Use the carrot-and-stick approach. The carrot: Tell the agent that if she brings you a listing that meets your criteria, you always will make an offer. Now, for that offer to be good for the agent, the buyer has to put enough down to pay the commission.

Carefully explain what you are looking for. Tell agents that you are looking for an empty house or a house owned by sellers who need to sell this week. Anyone who owns an empty house is getting no benefit from it and probably is worrying about it. These sellers are the most motivated to sell.

BUYING BIGGER EQUITIES

When I started my investment career, I would look for houses where the price listed was just the commission amount above the loan balance. My reasoning was that these sellers probably were having trouble making their payments because they would get nothing from the sale but relief from the loan. When I made offers on these houses, there was never enough money to pay a full commission.

There are two weaknesses with this strategy. First, you rarely buy far below the market. Second, the agent doesn't remember you fondly because it is unlikely that he was paid a full commission.

A better strategy is to tell agents that you are looking for houses with bigger equities. This will give you more room to negotiate a better price, and it increases the chance that the agent would get paid a full commission.

Stress that you have the ability to make a quick decision and could close the sale in a week or less. This will get you a lot of calls in the last days of the listing period (a great time to make an offer—both the seller and the broker are under pressure to make a deal).

The stick in the carrot-and-stick approach is this: Tell agents that when you find a desperate seller and the broker with the listing has not called you, then the offer may not include enough cash to pay the commission. This is subtle, but they get it.

WHO TO CALL WHEN YOU WANT TO BUY A LISTING

Most of us know a number of real estate brokers and salespeople. When you spot a house or an ad for a house that has potential, it is a mistake to call a friend. If they want to get paid, they should be looking for these deals and calling you.

When you find a potential bargain, call the listing agent. I wrote about this earlier. The agent will receive two shares of the commission if she sells her own listing. This extra incentive to put the deal together will have this agent working twice as hard to get it closed.

I made a $170,000 offer on a house listed for $225,000. I eventually raised my offer to $175,000, still short of what the seller needed to pay off the loan and pay closing costs. The listing agent agreed to pitch in part of her commission to make the deal work.

PAYING AGENTS WHEN THERE IS NO CASH FOR A COMMISSION

Sometimes there is not enough cash in the transaction to pay a commission. Most residential brokers are hoping for a check at the closing. When there is no money to pay them a cash commission, promise to pay them later, perhaps when you resell the property. You can back your promise to pay with a promissory note secured by either the property you are buying or another property that you already own.

Some brokers make a lot of money. They avoid investing because it is too much trouble. If you make investing easy for them, you may be able to turn things around and collect a check from them at the closing rather than write them one.

Keep in mind that in a normal market, 70 percent of listings expire before they sell. If the agent is convinced that this one will not sell, he will be eager to make some deal to get paid something for his efforts, advertising, and so on.

One thing Warren Harding taught me was to follow the cash in a transaction. Agents often buy the new buyer a gift and stay in touch with him. Wrong strategy. The buyer is broke. He just spent it all on the house. Follow the seller or the agent. They have cash in their pocket and may be potential investors.

BUYING ON LEASE OPTIONS THROUGH AGENTS

Often the best offer to make on a house is to lease it with an option to buy. How do you pay the broker when you are making a low down payment such as an option payment? Offer to pay the agent part of the fee when the lease/option agreement is signed and the balance at the actual closing.

You can go a step further and say to the agent and the seller that if you do not close on the purchase, the seller would agree to relist the property with the same agent when the option expires. In this way, the agent gets part of a commission now and will get another full commission when he sells it again.

Suppose that a house is listed for $140,000, and you offer to lease it for four years paying $5,000 down as option consideration today. A 7 percent commission is $9,800. If the agent received 25 percent of that commission, or $2,450 today, with the balance paid when you exercise the option, this is still far better than not selling the house at all. If the seller is more anxious than the agent, then the agent may negotiate for more of the option payment.

USING THE DIFFERENT TYPES OF LISTINGS

The two commonly used types of listings are an *open listing* and *an exclusive right of sale.* An open listing is typically unwritten. With an open listing, the owner agrees to pay the broker only if she produces a sale.

An exclusive listing guarantees the agent a commission if the property sells during the term of the listing regardless of who buys. Exclusive listings are required by Multiple Listing Systems (MLS) and many of the big brokers. Many exclusive listings can obligate a seller to pay a commission to the agent if anyone they showed the house to (or even told about it) buys the house within a specified period after the listing expires. Read these listings carefully before you ever sign one or make an offer on a house bound by one.

A seller can exclude specific buyers, even from an exclusive listing. If you are interested in a house that a seller is going to list with an agent, have the seller exclude you from that listing. Then, if you buy, there will be no obligation to pay a commission.

Another type of listing, the *exclusive agency listing,* allows the owner to avoid paying a commission if he sells it himself but protects one agent in the event another agent sells it. It is not used as commonly because MLS generally will not accept properties listed this way.

If you ever list a property, use an exclusive listing to get the benefit of MLS exposure. You want every hotshot selling agent in town showing your house. Agree to pay the highest commission common in your area. The difference between 6 and 7 percent is not as important as selling the house quickly.

Insist on a short-term agreement. A 90-day listing is as long as I would suggest. Read the fine print carefully, and remember to exclude any buyers with whom you are now negotiating. Be wary of accepting offers that are subject to the buyers obtaining financing or selling another house before they close on yours. These offers take your house off the market without compensation to you. If you do want to accept an offer subject to one of these contingencies, use one of these strategies:

1. State that in the event that you receive another offer acceptable to you, the buyers will have the right to waive their contingency and close within 30 days or void the contract.
2. Ask for a nonrefundable deposit of $1,000 that the buyers forfeit if they fail to close. This money will compensate you for taking the property off the market for a month. If the buyers need longer, ask for more money.

BROKERS CAN BE GOOD CUSTOMERS

Not all agents are rolling in dough. In fact, only the top producers make any serious money. Most are average consumers, struggling to pay their mortgage and car payments. I have both sold houses to and bought houses from such agents.

Many agents have trouble qualifying for a loan because their income is from commissions and is not predictable. In addition, some have credit problems. They are good candidates for a lease/option or owner-financing sale. Recently, I sold two houses that needed quite of bit of work to agents on lease/options. They can fix them up and then refinance them and pay me off.

I've bought many homes from agents. One broker has sold me his personal residence twice. When times are good, he buys a nice home, but he never gets emotionally attached to it. When cash gets tight, he knows that I will buy it and gives me a call. He knows that when he can't borrow, he can sell.

As you develop trust with agents, they become repeat customers. They will bring you sellers or buyers and sometimes just refer business to you. An agent can't make money from a buyer who has little money or credit. But that buyer may make a good tenant for you or even a lease/option buyer.

Likewise, an agent can't collect a commission from a seller who is behind on her payments and has no equity. However, you may know how to buy that house, save the seller's credit, and make a profit. I have had several calls referring these desperate sellers to me by agents.

ADVICE TO AGENTS WHO BUY PROPERTY

If you are a Realtor, *don't* buy your own listings. You are the agent for the seller and cannot ethically make a good deal. Cancel any and all listings, whether written or implied, before making an offer. If you buy your own listing and either deduct your commission or receive it at the closing and later resell the property for a profit, you are likely to be sued by the seller. The seller will claim that all you are entitled to is a commission, but you made more. Therefore, the seller is entitled to the overage (plus attorney's fees and costs).

Don't pay taxes on your own money. When you make a down payment and then collect a commission at the closing, you are just getting part of your down payment back. Unfortunately, any commission you receive is taxable income to you.

Likewise, if you trade services for a down payment, the services you trade can be classified as taxable income. If you forgo a commission and take equity in the property, you have still earned that commission, and it is still taxable. When buying, do not participate in any commission.

SHOULD YOU HAVE A REAL ESTATE LICENSE?

If all you do is buy for your own investment, the license is not necessary or even an advantage. An agent must disclose that he is licensed when making offers. I never found this to be a problem, although others have. A typical disclosure may read: "John Smith is a registered real estate broker in the state of Florida and is purchasing this property for his own account with the intention of making a profit. Smith will not participate in any commissions paid in this transaction. Any listing, whether written, oral, or implied, between Smith and the seller is hereby voided. Sellers are advised to seek legal advice."

The education available to agents is an advantage, although it is often designed to make you a better agent, not a better investor. If you do not have a license, don't get one unless you want to work as an agent and collect commissions.

If you now have a license and it does not have a negative impact on your investing, keep it until it does. Most sellers in a hurry would rather do business with someone in business—someone who knows how to fill out a contract, someone who does not have to go to a bank and beg for money, someone who will really buy their house. Having a license is not a hindrance when you are buying from someone who really needs to sell.

10

BUYING AND SELLING HOUSES TO PRODUCE CASH FLOW—NOW

Buying and selling a house for a quick profit is exciting work and can produce significant short-term cash flow. This is different from investing in a house and holding it for long-term profit.

The business of buying and selling requires certain skills and takes a serious commitment of time. Many people who attempt this strategy are unsuccessful because they underestimate the amount of skill and time it takes to buy and sell for a profit.

Buying and holding a house for a long-tem profit requires less skill because time is on your side. You can buy a house at a retail price, and if you hold it long enough, you will make a profit. The longer you hold a property in a good location, the more money you will make.

As an investor, you will acquire the skills you need as you research your area, talk to hundreds (yes, hundreds) of sellers, and negotiate and close deals.

When you have the needed skills, you can buy some houses for investment and others to increase your cash flow today. If you are trying to transition from working for someone else to being a full-time real estate investor, buying and selling a couple of houses a year can give you the cash you will need for down payments and living expenses.

If you are already a full-time investor, you are constantly looking for good deals. You will find houses that do not meet your criteria as an investment property. Rather than just passing on such a property, buy and sell it for a profit.

To qualify as a good long-term investment, a house should be well designed and well built and, most important, be in a neighborhood that will attract long-term tenants and appreciate at an above-average rate.

When you are buying and selling houses for short-term profit, time works against you. It may take you several months to find and buy a good deal. After you close on the deal, every day you own it the holding costs (interest, taxes, insurance, advertising, repairs) reduce your profit. To make a profit, you need to sell before your profits are eaten up by your holding costs.

Your annual profit from buying and selling houses depends on two factors:

1. How far below the market you buy each house
2. How many houses you are able to buy a year

Some investors buy multiple houses but make only a little on each house. Others buy just a few houses and make a larger profit per house.

ANNUAL PROFIT = PROFIT PER HOUSE × NUMBER OF HOUSES BOUGHT AND SOLD

The key to making a profit is buying a house at a below-market price and then reselling as quickly as possible. You cannot sell a house in a short time at an above-market price. The higher the price, the longer it will take to sell. The amount of profit you will make will depend on how far below market you can buy the house.

If you can find a good deal once in one month, close the purchase and fix it up in one month, and sell and close it in just one more month (an incredibly optimistic time table), you are on track to buy and sell four houses a year. If your goal is to make $60,000 a year, you need to net $15,000 profit per house.

This is a good strategy if you are a skilled buyer and able to invest time and energy to the work and able to buy below the market consistently. Many people who attempt this, who buy and sell, are not accomplished negotiators and buyers. They buy marginal deals and try to make a profit by selling at above-market prices.

You want to be good at buying and selling for more reasons than just making money. The more houses you buy and sell in a year, the more you have to work and the more risks you take. You want to be skillful enough and professional enough in your work to make your efforts worthwhile and insulate you from litigation.

Many legal issues arise and a good number of lawsuits result from buy/sell transactions that go amiss. The other party (it could be either the buyer or the seller) feels that she has been taken advantage of, or a flaw in the property surfaces after the closing. Sometimes these issues can only be resolved with a lawsuit, but you want to make that a rare adventure and not a likely outcome of your real estate hobby.

SIX STEPS TO MAKING MONEY BUYING AND SELLING HOUSES

1. *Identify the price range of houses in your town that sells the fastest.* You want to buy houses to resell in this price range. A Realtor can give you this information. Typically, it is a house you would call a starter house or one step above that house. It is often just below the median-priced house in a town. Often there is a large inventory of these houses, and although there is competition to buy, these houses are easier to sell.

A cardinal rule of real estate is that it is easier to buy than to sell. When you are the buyer, you are in control. You can choose how much to offer and decide whether to buy or pass. When you are selling, you can lower your price and offer terms to attract buyers, but you cannot make them buy. You can lead a buyer to a good deal, but you can't make them buy.

2. *Identify several neighborhoods that have houses for sale in the price range you want to buy and sell.* Look for signs of opportunity. An empty house always signals opportunity to me. Not all empty houses are opportunities, but most opportunities are empty houses.

An owner with an empty house will be more eager to sell than an owner who is still living in the house or has the house rented. Some houses are occupied but not rented. Either the tenants have quit paying rent and the landlord has done nothing to correct the problem, or sometimes a relative or friend has moved into a house to "house sit" or take care of it until it sells.

If the tenant or "house sitter" is not a good house and yard keeper, it detracts from the house and makes it harder to sell. This is a sign of opportunity.

Look for any house that is not well maintained. If the owner cannot afford to paint it, fix a leaking roof, or keep the yard up, it may be a sign that he needs to sell.

Walk the streets in the neighborhoods that interest you. Look carefully at each house on the street. You will notice a lot that you would not see driving the street. Talk to the neighbors. Knock on doors and ask if they know of any houses in the neighborhood for sale. This is the most effective way to find a good deal.

Good deals are rarely listed.

Most houses that are opportunities are not even for sale. There will be no sign in the yard and no ad in the paper. Many people in trouble simply hope that their problem will solve itself and take no action to solve it. This is why walking through a neighborhood and knocking on doors is such an effective way to find a good deal.

3. *Once you find a good deal, research it.* Find out what the owner paid and what others have paid for similar houses on the street recently.

4. *Now set a minimum profit goal.* A more expensive house that may be harder to resell should command a larger profit. Likewise, a house that needs considerable work and will consume a lot of your time and money needs to produce a larger profit.

For a beginning buyer, a profit goal of 10 percent of the purchase price is a good minimum target. It is low enough that you can buy properties consistently and develop the confidence and negotiating skills that you need. You will develop better buying skills as you negotiate for more property.

5. *Start keeping a journal.* Every time you buy a house, write down in your journal the following points:

- Why you thought that this house would be a good deal
- How you came up with your first offer
- How the buyer responded to the offer
- What the offer was that was accepted
- What you would offer if you could start over

Before you make your next offer, review the last offer that you had accepted and try to make this next offer a little better for you. As you become more skilled, increase your profit per house goal. Experienced buyers command 20 percent or greater discounts when they buy.

If you are willing to work for less than a 10 percent discount, get a real estate license and collect a commission. You don't have to take the risk, make a down payment, or pay the carrying costs that being in the buy/sell business requires. In the process of getting a license, you will learn the laws that regulate agents in your state. Hopefully, you will learn about contracts, deeds, closing statements, title insurance, and other facets of the real estate business.

Taking the course, even if you don't want a license, will teach you more about the process of buying and selling. Licensed agents need to disclose that they have a license in the contract when buying and should never take a commission when buying. By taking a commission when you buy, you are being paid by the sellers to be their agent. When you are buying, you are not representing the sellers' best interests; you are trying to get the best price for yourself. Taking a commission is inviting a lawsuit.

If you intend to receive a 10 percent return on your money (and consider a return on your time as well), then you need to work on your skills and devote the time required to buy and sell houses for profit. The 10 and 20 percent figures are just profit targets. Anyone who actually has bought and sold a property will tell you that you don't always make as much as you plan to make. Sometimes you get lucky and make more, but it often takes longer to sell or costs more to make repairs than you planned, and your profit is less than your target.

A REALTOR WHO WORKED FOR LESS THAN A COMMISSION

A Realtor bought a house from me that needed updating. I had owned it for about 10 years and had rented it to the same tenant for that entire time. The house had more than doubled in value, and the Realtor made me an offer I did not refuse.

She fixed it up and sold it several months later for about a $5,000 gross profit (not counting her holding costs or taxes). She would have made more money listing and selling it without spending the time and investing the money to fix it up and market it.

You can make more than $5,000 per house when you buy and sell, but there are no guarantees. Other investors have sold houses to me for less than they paid after trying unsuccessfully to sell for a profit.

A long-term investor can wait patiently for a strong market, keeping a house rented until the time is right to sell, and harvest a large profit. A short-term "flipper" does not have that luxury.

After you buy a house at a bargain price, you have to sell it for more than you paid for it, plus your holding costs, plus any money you have to invest to improve the house. Short-term profits you make from buying and selling are subject to the higher tax rates applied to ordinary income, not the capital gains rate available on investment property gains.

Taxes will become a greater concern once you begin to make a lot of money. Learn to make money first, and then learn how to reduce your taxes. If you are broke, you don't need a good tax strategy or asset-protection plan. You need assets and income.

Once your taxable income from buying and selling exceeds $30,000 a year, talk with a certified public accountant (CPA) who owns real estate himself about options that can reduce your tax liability. Using a corporation or limited-liability company (LLC) to buy and sell properties can reduce your tax bill and give you some liability protection. There are both advantages and disadvantages to using an entity to buy and sell, so get good advice before you spend the money to form one.

WHICH HOUSES TO BUY AND WHICH HOUSES NOT TO BUY

There are some houses you should not buy at any price. There are houses that are beyond repair at a reasonable cost (unless you are buying at below the lot value) and houses in neighborhoods where there are no owner occupants and no trend toward more owner occupants. When a neighborhood is entirely owned by landlords, your only buyers will be other landlords. You might be able to sell to them at a profit, but they will be tough negotiators, and often these pros will want you to finance the property.

The ideal house to buy is one in a neighborhood with many owner occupants who maintain their property, a neighborhood where buyers will want to live and will pay a retail price when they buy. A house that needs only a little work is better to buy than one that needs a total rehab. The more work a house needs, the more money you will have to invest and the longer it will take you to make a profit.

SELLING HOUSES THAT NEED WORK IN "AS IS" CONDITION

I have had considerable experience in remodeling and repairing properties before I resell them. I do this with experienced and skilled full-time employees so that I can keep my costs low and I don't have to wait for contractors to show up to do work.

Even with the advantage of being able to do work "in house," I still find that in many cases I make more money selling houses that need work to a buyer in "as is" condition rather than doing the work myself.

CASE STUDY: THE HOUSE OF THE RISING WATER

I bought a house from a bank that had neglected to maintain it. The bank had allowed a roof to leak for months during the rainy season, and the water in the house was getting deeper by the week. The ceilings had fallen in, the kitchen cabinets had fallen off the walls, and all the drywall was soaked.

This house needed work!

I put together the following projection of the cost to buy and repair the house and then to sell it:

Purchase price:	$90,000
Estimated cost of repairs:	$50,000
Time to make repairs:	2 months
Time to market and close:	2 months
Estimated holding and marketing costs:	$5,000
Total projected investment:	$145,000
Estimate selling price:	$189,000
Projected profit before taxes:	$44,000

Once I had a contract to buy the house from the bank, I put a for sale sign in the yard. I had several calls because many buyers are looking for bargains that need work. There was one family who wanted to buy the house but did not have enough money or credit to buy it; however, they did have the ability and resources to do the work needed. *Never sell a house that needs work to a buyer unless the buyer can convince you that he can do the work needed.*

I agreed to sell them the house on a one-year lease/option contract in "as is" condition with a $1,000 down payment at a price of $120,000. I gave the buyers three months' reduced rent ($100 a month) and had them agree in the written contract specifically what work they would do during that three months.

Their plan was to get the house in livable condition in the first three months. Working with friends from their church, they were able to clean out the house, repair it, move in, and get it financed at a bank with an appraisal of $189,000 within six months. They borrowed enough money to pay me in full and recover most of their expenses.

The results:

My purchase price:	$90,000
My cost of repairs:	$0
Time to market and close:	6 months
Actual holding costs:	$3,000
(I collected 3 months' rent)	
Total investment:	$93,000
Selling price:	$120,000
Profit before taxes:	$27,000

Although I made less money, I significantly reduced my risk and time invested. If the buyers had not closed on their contract, I would have owned a much better house than I turned over to them.

When you have a house that needs this much work, typically you go over budget on both time and money. When you can take an acceptable profit and let someone else take the responsibility for the work, you free up your time to look for the next good deal. You also eliminate or at least reduce your risk.

Selling a house with a small down payment has risks. If the house needs a lot of work and your buyers do some or all of that work, the work they contribute is the equivalent of a bigger down payment. If a house needs no work, require a larger cash down payment. If the sale falls through, you need enough cash to make any needed repairs to the house and remarket it.

11

SELLING ON LEASE/OPTIONS TO GENERATE THE LARGEST PROFITS

To make a great buy, you typically have to sign a contract to buy the house today and then close within a few days. The reason people sell houses for far less than what they are worth is because they have to: They don't have enough time to wait for a retail buyer.

When you sell a house, if you sell to a buyer who cannot close right away—who needs some time to pay you—you can sell for a significantly higher price. I often make an additional $10,000 per house when I sell on a short-term lease/option contract.

In the case of the "house of the rising water" discussed in Chapter 10, I sold the house using a lease/option contract. A lease/option is a form of owner financing but a simpler, safer, and less costly way to sell to a buyer who may not be able to qualify for a loan.

Most buyers who want owner financing cannot qualify for a bank loan. There are always a substantial number of house buyers—or would-be buyers—who cannot qualify for a bank loan because of poor credit or low income. Some owner wannabes are eager to buy and are willing to pay a retail price and make regular payments if they are given the opportunity.

Using a lease/option, I sell many families their first home. They pay an option payment and then monthly lease payments for the term of the contract. If they want to buy the house, they must at some point qualify for a bank loan.

QUALIFIYING YOUR BUYERS

Before I sell to them, I get financial information and identify why they cannot qualify today for a loan. I help them to form a plan so that they can qualify within a period of time, often one or two years. If they have too many expenses, often the solution is to pay off a credit card debt or a car loan—and to avoid new debt. If they have poor credit because of overdue bills, I counsel them to form a plan to pay off those bills and then to begin making timely payments on their other credit accounts.

SETTING THE OPTION PAYMENT, THE RENT, AND THE PRICE

The option payment, the monthly rental amount, and the price you'll sell the house for are directly related. You can charge a higher sales price if you will accept a lower option payment and rent. However, if no one ever buys because your price is too high, then you will never sell the house.

Which of the three—option payment, rent, or price—has the greatest impact on your total profit? If you increase the option payment from $3,000 to $5,000, how does that affect your profit? If the optionee doesn't buy, you get to keep a larger option payment, but if the optionee does buy, you make the same amount of profit.

Raising the monthly rent will produce more income, but you must balance the amount of rent you charge with how long it will take you to rent the house. If you try to get an extra $100 a month, and the house sits empty for a month, you probably have lost more than you can recover. Using a lower rent and renting faster often will make you more money.

Of the three variables, the price is the one that will have the greatest impact on your profit. If you make someone a good deal on the rent and accept a relatively small option deposit, but set your price at the top of the retail range, you will collect several thousands of dollars more in profit when you close.

GETTING THE BEST PRICE WHEN YOU SELL

Table 11.1 presents an example of what you may be able to charge for a house in a typical market, one appreciating from 3 to 6 percent. Notice that both the price and rent are expressed in ranges. It is impossible to put an exact price or rent on a house. If you had four appraisers give you a price, you would get four different prices. You need to know your market well enough that you can establish these ranges. Establish a range for both price and rent that allows you to form a strategy for selling.

Selling on lease/options is an art, not a science. Every house will have a different market appeal: Some will need lots of work, and others will be ready to move into. The desirability of the neighborhood will determine how many people will want the house and how much they are willing to pay. Table 11.1 shows the relationship between what

Table 11.1 Reducing the Rent and Deposit to Get the Highest Price

Today's retail house value:	$150,000–$160,000
Today's market rent:	$1,100–$1,200
Market conditions:	Appreciation of 3%–6%

Price	Option Payment	Rent
$170,000	$2,000	$1,050
$165,000	$3,000	$1,100
$160,000	$4,000	$1,150
$155,000	$5,000	$1,200
$150,000	$7,500	$1,250
$145,000	$10,000	$1,300

price you ask, what rent you ask, and the amount of option money you are able to command.

Notice which number has the greatest impact on your profit—it's the price. By charging a lower rent and deposit, you can charge a higher price. The amount of the deposit you charge will have an impact on the number of buyers who actually close. The lower the deposit you charge, the fewer will be the number of sellers who actually close on the purchase.

A buyer with more money and better credit is likely to be a better negotiator and often will negotiate the sales price. If you can sell at a higher price and still collect a larger down payment, do it. It is probably a sign that the market is heating up and that prices will be moving up faster.

The time it takes you to sell the house will be determined by how you price it. If you ask for a high price, high rent, and a high deposit, it may take you months to sell. In an average market, you can sell a house on a lease/option in a month or less if you price it at retail and charge a fair rent and deposit.

If getting a higher price is more important to you than getting more rent or more money up front, then you should advertise the house with a lower down payment and rent to make it more attractive to more buyers.

If getting your money sooner is more important to you, then selling at a lower price and getting a larger deposit will increase the chance of the buyers actually closing. The more they have invested up front, the harder they will work to close on the house.

The option payment is part of the money you are asking for before you give a lease/option buyer possession of the house. You also will collect the first month's rent—in cash. The total amount you collect needs to be low enough to attract buyers. The condition of the house and the desirability of the house will determine how much you can charge.

Bob Bruss advises to advertise the amount of money it takes to move you in:

Lease/option:	$5,000 moves you in
Quaint 3/2/2 on quiet street:	$399,000
Call Bob at 222-2222	

Bob invests in the San Francisco area and sells houses in high price ranges on lease/options with relatively small down payments.

DON'T USE LEASE/OPTIONS AS A MANGEMENT TOOL

Some lease/option sellers never actually sell a house. They sign a lease/option to renters who could never qualify for a loan. These sellers are just collecting additional money in the form of option payments every time they rent the property.

Use a lease/option to sell a house that you want to sell. Don't use it as a technique to increase your cash flow from your long-term investments. There are risks to selling your investment houses on lease/options. First, if the market takes off and prices jump 15 to 20 percent in one year, many of your buyers will buy. This will take you out of the market just when you want to own property.

Suppose that you owned 10 houses and instead of renting them, you sold them all on lease/options to increase your cash flow and reduce your maintenance costs. (Later, in the section on management, you will learn how to rent to tenants who will take care of your property.)

House prices jump 20 percent, and 8 of 10 of your tenants buy their houses, leaving you with a large tax bill to pay or the challenge of reinvesting your money in property in a market that's going up 20 percent a year. If the houses were worth an average of $200,000, you have given up (20% × $200,000) or about $40,000 per house profit.

The lease/option is the best way to sell a property at a retail price, but don't make the mistake of selling property that you want to keep. When you buy a house in a strong neighborhood with good long-term financing, don't sell it just because someone wants to buy it. Your best houses will make you the most money. Others constantly will try to buy them from you.

SETTING THE TERM, MONTHLY CREDIT, AND EXTENSIONS

When you sell a house, use a one-year lease/option period. If house prices jump 10 percent during the year, you are giving less away when you use a short term. If the buyers are nervous (and they often are) that one year may not be enough time for them to solve the problem that keeps them from qualifying for a loan, then offer them a one-year extension—at a higher price. In an average market, use a 5 percent increase in both the price and the rent for the second year. If the market is increasing at a faster rate, ask for a larger increase. You always can give some of the increase back if you want to sell the house and it does not appraise at the higher price when the buyers apply for a loan.

Put in your lease/option agreement a monthly credit amount toward the purchase that the buyers will "receive" when they pay on time. Use $100 a month. If you use a higher amount, the lender who the buyers borrow from may disallow it unless they are paying a credit on top of the fair market rent. While a larger credit may make the buyers more interested in buying the house, it will not help them to get a loan. If they accumulate a large credit and then cannot buy the house, they may feel entitled to part of it if they cannot buy.

BEING A GOOD GUY IF THEY CANNOT BUY

Reporters have asked me what percentage of my lease/option buyers actually close. Overall, it's about 50 percent, but it depends on the credit market. When interest rates are low and loans are easier to come by, the percentage of buyers who can qualify for a loan and close goes way up—to 100 percent in some years. When interest rates rise and loans are hard to get unless you have perfect credit, then the percentage of buyers drops.

When that happens, I often renegotiate the agreement so that the buyers can stay in the house and continue to try to buy it. I adjust the rent and price to keep up with the market. Eventually, if the buyers clean up their credit, they can buy the house.

In the event that the buyers change their mind, get transferred, or get divorced, sick, or any of the real-world things that happen to people every day, then I offer some of their original deposit back if they have paid the rent and taken care of the property. In effect, I treat them like a good tenant and refund part of their original option money, treating it like a security deposit.

This is a nice thing to do, and it is also good business. If you have to go through the eviction process to move out a tenant who was buying under a lease/option, it will cost you both your time and money. It is better business to give the buyers some of their own money back as an incentive to move and give you back a house in good condition than to use the courts to force them out.

If you get a house back in good condition, then you can resell it quickly to another lease/option tenant.

GETTING YOUR CASH NOW WHEN YOU SELL ON LEASE/OPTIONS

When you buy a house that you intend to sell on a lease/option, you may need to recover part of the cash that you have tied up in the house before the buyers close on their lease/option contract. A bank line of credit and a private line of credit are good ways to obtain the cash you need before you receive your profit.

Suppose that you bought and sold this house:

Market value today:	$170,000–$180,000
Your purchase price:	$150,000
Your down payment:	$30,000
Your loan:	$120,000
You resell on a lease/option:	
Sale price:	$179,900
Option payment	$5,000
Balance due:	$174,900
Your loan balance	$120,000 (This will be adjusted at closing to include any monthly credits the buyers have earned.)
Your equity in the contract:	$54,900

You now have about $55,000 of equity in the contract and about $25,000 cash tied up in the house (your $30,000 down payment less the $5,000 down payment). You can use this contract to borrow $25,000 on a short-term loan either from a bank or from a private party. You can show the lender that she will be repaid from the proceeds at the closing. You could assign your contract as collateral for the loan if she insists, but often you can borrow unsecured. If the house does not close as planned, you will sell it again and pay off your loan when it does close.

If you are getting the money from a private investor, you could sell her a half interest in your equity in the house, subject to the lease/option sale, for $25,000. The investor would then own one-half the house and would receive one-half the rent as well as the proceeds ($54,900/2 = $27,450) when the sale closes. If the first sale does not close, then you would resell the house at hopefully a higher price, and the investor would then participate in half that sale.

A BUSINESS PLAN FOR BUYING AND SELLING

If you want to make buying and selling a full-time business, you need a plan to produce a certain amount of income. Here is a simple plan that you can use as a format to form your own plan. Plug in real numbers in your town to see how it would work for you.

Annual income goal:	$80,000
Price range of houses that will sell quickly:	$140,000–$150,000
Projected average profit per house (year one):	$20,000
Number of houses needed to meet income goal:	4
Average down payment required to buy a house:	$20,000
Average option payment received when selling:	$5,000
Cash needed to buy first house:	$20,000

Borrowing against the first contract could raise the down payment for the second house. With $80,000 in initial capital, you could acquire all four houses without borrowing.

Compare this business with other small businesses that you could own and operate in your town. Most small businesses require far more than $80,000 in startup capital. They also require employees, and have overhead such as rent, advertising, utilities, and so on. Many businesses have inventory that can spoil (like food), go out of style (like shoes), or be stolen. Your inventory is appreciating, won't go out of style, and it's hard to steal.

The owner of a small business often works or is on call many hours, seven days a week; in addition to his own work, such an owner must supervise the work of his employees. You alone, working part time, can generate more net income than most small businesses in your town.

DOING GOOD WORK AND GETTING PAID FOR IT

The business of buying and selling houses provides a service to your community. There are always sellers who need to sell quickly and buyers with credit problems who need help buying. By treating people fairly and by filling both these needs, you can make a good living and help people out of difficult situations. At the same time, you can hold onto the better properties for long-term investment, which will one day give you the ability simply to collect rent rather than continue to buy and sell.

12

FINDING AND BUYING PREFORECLOSURES AND FORECLOSURES

Buying property from an owner in distress is exciting and can be very profitable. However, it is often complicated and requires specialized knowledge of the system and the law.

If you are a beginning investor, read this chapter, but know that you need some experience before you have success buying foreclosures. When you find an opportunity, use a competent real estate attorney who can guide you through the process of buying your first foreclosure. Another investor may be able to refer you to a knowledgeable attorney.

HOW AND WHY FORECLOSURES OCCUR

It is easy to borrow money against a home you own. Sometimes it is too easy, and homeowners borrow more than they can afford to repay. When this happens and the borrower stops making payments, both the lender and the homeowner have a problem.

Most lenders do not want to foreclose a loan and take title to a property. They are not property managers; they are lenders. Often, when they foreclose, they lose money on the loan. They cannot sell the property for enough to recover the loan balance and cost.

When a borrower loses a house in foreclosure, the event has a long-lasting effect on the borrower's credit. When the borrower is able to borrow money again, it will be at a much higher interest rate. Banks will be reluctant to make another home loan to that borrower for many years.

Even more distressing is loss of the family home and the need to move abruptly into less of a house in a weaker neighborhood. This is traumatic to a family and can cause other family problems. If you can offer a solution to this serious financial problem, you can save the homeowner a lot of grief and money and personally make a substantial profit for your skill and efforts.

Foreclosures can result from misfortune, such as an accident, illness, or a job layoff. More often they are a result of a homeowner borrowing money on terms he cannot afford. Regardless of the reason for the foreclosure, the key to buying a property from an owner facing foreclosure is how you deal with the owner and the problem.

BEWARE OF THE FORECLOSURE SHARKS

Some people who buy properties in foreclosure are not tactful or even ethical. Buyers who use high-pressure tactics to get sellers who are behind in their payments to sign a contact may be breaking the law. Buyers who "steal" property, leaving nothing on the table for the sellers, don't get many referrals or make many friends.

BUYING FORECLOSURES AND MAKING FRIENDS WHILE DOING IT

There is a different approach to buying properties in foreclosure. After 30 years of buying houses, nearly all my business is referrals. Previous sellers, borrowers, buyers, renters, and agents call me with repeat business and send me their friends. You can buy property from owners in distress and leave them with their honor intact and happy that they did business with you. The secret: Deal with others as you would like to be treated if you were in their situation, and solve the problem.

NOT ALL FORECLOSURES ARE OPPORTUNITIES

Some property in foreclosure—as with property in general—is not worth buying because of its bad location or poor condition. Some owners are just too difficult to help or to make a deal with. Do not stray from your investment plan just to buy a property in foreclosure. Only look at houses in price ranges and in neighborhoods that you understand and that you know are profitable.

Often properties are in foreclosure because of a bad location, bad design, or bad concept. These problems may be expensive or even impossible to fix. If you buy these properties, even at a bargain price, you may become the next owner in distress. Frequently you will see the same house foreclosed on several times—there is a problem with that house, not just the owners.

FIVE SOURCES OF DELINQUENT HOMEOWNERS WHO NEED YOU

1. *Homeowners who are in trouble and still trying to borrow more money.* When a homeowner falls behind on her first mortgage, she often will try to borrow more against the house from a second mortgage lender to catch up the payments on the first. These second mortgages are recorded in the public records and can be a source of leads.

Some lenders are much more aggressive than others and will make higher-risk loans. While most lenders want a certain level of credit and income, some lenders will loan to nearly anyone with income, even if that person is behind on his first loan and jobless.

Learn who the most aggressive lenders are in your area, and recognize that only the most desperate borrowers will borrow from them. Their interest rates and upfront fees will be high—and so will their default rate. If these borrowers were in financial trouble before, borrowing more money at a high interest rate will only compound their trouble.

When you identify these borrowers, you are identifying people who may need to sell their house soon—and in a hurry.

You can identify these borrowers by searching the public records for loans recorded by these high-risk lenders and then contacting the borrowers. Simply tell them that you are looking for a house in their neighborhood, and ask them if they know anyone who wants to sell. This low-key approach opens the door to asking more questions if they admit that they want to sell.

Another direct approach is to meet with the people making these loans. They are paid on commission when they make a loan. You can offer them a finder's fee to refer homeowners to you who need to sell, not borrow more. Even the most aggressive lenders turn down some homeowners because they have too much debt already. These homeowners may have little equity, but the lenders they owe may be willing to renegotiate the terms of their loans, allowing you to buy for a profit.

2. *A second source of owners in trouble is an ad.*

Cash for Your House

Fast Closing

Save Your Equity

Call John anytime at 222-2222

If you have many ads like this in your paper, run an ad under mortgages wanted or money to lend that reads:

Private Investor Has Cash

for Notes and Mortgages

Call John anytime at 222-2222

This ad will get calls from people looking for a loan. Both these ads will generate many leads. Your challenge will be screening them and following up on the good leads. Be sure to use a phone number that you can answer often; many of these people will not leave a callback number.

3. *A third source of homeowners in trouble is other house buyers.* If your newspaper is like mine, it usually has several ads that state, "I will buy your house for cash." The buyers running these ads can only buy so many. I have found that everyone seems to have a favorite type of house and a favorite neighborhood. The secret is to find another buyer who is

short on cash or has an interest different from yours and offer to pay him for leads on the houses that you like.

4. *A fourth source is referrals from bankers and other lenders whom you may know.* Local lenders often refer troubled homeowners to other lenders; when such homeowners are in too much trouble to borrow more, they refer them to buyers.

Understand that lenders will not call you and tell you about their customer. They will call their customers and tell them about you. To get these referrals, the lender must first know that you buy houses and then trust that you will treat people fairly. Lenders do not want negative repercussions from referring you business.

5. *A fifth source is property in good neighborhoods that is being neglected.* I frequently drive and walk through neighborhoods I like looking for empty or physically distressed property. While not every property that needs work is an opportunity, it is a free phone call to the owners to find out if they want to sell. Even if you only buy one in a hundred and it takes you three months to find one that you can buy, this is highly profitable work.

There are more sources, but this is enough to get you started. *The key is you.* You need to do research, make contacts, run ads, and canvass neighborhoods to generate the leads that you need. There are always opportunities.

TALKING WITH OWNERS IN FORECLOSURE

Many owners in foreclosure are not willing to answer questions or even admit that they have a problem. Try to help them, but only spend a little time with them unless they admit to needing help and are willing to accept it.

Explain the consequences of a foreclosure:

1. Poor credit will cause them to pay higher interest rates.
2. They may have to move into a much less desirable house.
3. They may not have enough money to move into any house.
4. They will lose their equity.
5. A new job or a promotion may require a credit check. An applicant who is under severe financial stress may not be a desirable employee.
6. A foreclosure can be a long-term family disaster.

TESTING THE OWNER'S MOTIVATION

Most sellers want you to come to look at their house. As a test of their motivation and willingness to cooperate, ask a homeowner in distress to come to you. Ask her to bring all her paperwork on the house.

Specifically ask for loan documents, title insurance, closing documents from the purchase, and any refinancing and all correspondence from the lender or lenders. These documents will give you the information you need to assess the situation and consider if you are part of a solution. A solution would be to make the owner an offer if you can make a profit in a transaction that solves her problem.

GIVING SOUND ADVICE TO DELINQUENT BORROWERS

Borrowing more money is not a solution when you cannot make your current payments. Unless you can roll the back payments into a new loan with a lower payment, you are just getting deeper in trouble. Refinancing loans in default is expensive and often has high closing costs and high interest rates. It may buy a little time, but often at a high cost.

If the house has enough equity to refinance, it has enough equity to sell. Selling may net the owners some cash, avoid a foreclosure, and give the owners some options they would not have if they were foreclosed.

Never lend money to anyone behind in his payments. First, it is not good for them. If they cannot make their payments now, how could they make new, higher payments? Second, there are complex laws in many states that protect homeowners who are in default from unscrupulous lenders. You may violate one of those laws even when you are trying to help.

BUYING A HOUSE FROM AN OWNER IN DEFAULT

Buying homes from owners in foreclosure is not as simple as it seems on late-night TV. Your first challenge is finding owners (1) who are behind in their payments, (2) who own a house that you want, and (3) who will agree to sell. Finding them is not difficult; getting them to make a good decision (to sell to you) can be. They did not get in financial trouble by making good decisions.

Another challenge is dealing with the lenders. In this era of megabanks, it's a challenge to find the right person to talk to. Many loans in default are owed to lenders who have made higher-risk second mortgage loans. These lenders often are eager to talk because they are in a risky position. Some of these lenders are private individuals who are just trying to recover their capital.

A third challenge is finding the money to fund these purchases. Foreclosure buying can require a lot of cash. Lenders often will want cash for their positions. Investors who will loan you money at decent rates and will coinvest in longer-term deals are a good source, along with home equity loans and lines of credit.

DEALING WITH THE LENDERS

When borrowers quit making their loan payments, the lender begins writing letters trying to inspire them to pay. Understand that lenders do not want the real estate. They want their money back. While some lenders do make a profit when they foreclose, many more lose money. Foreclosures are an expensive distraction from their main source of profits—lending money.

A junior lender, one who has made a second, third, or even fourth position (behind other loans), is taking a bigger risk and often will be more aggressive and more creative in collecting her money.

Many first mortgages are insured for nonpayment through the Federal Housing Administration (FHA) or Mortgage Guarantee Insurance Corporation (MGIC) or are guaranteed by Veterans Administration (VA), so the lender's risk is lower. Second mortgage lenders rarely have insurance, so they are more willing to accept a partial payment when a loan is in default.

SOLVING THE DELINQUENT OWNER'S BIGGEST PROBLEM

To homeowners facing foreclosure, ruined credit and loss of equity are both small problems compared with having to move their family out of their home. They are facing a move into a rental house in a neighborhood that probably is far less desirable than their current one. An owner who has to move because of a foreclosure is no catch as a tenant and may have to accept the dregs of the rental market. Obviously, if an owner did not pay the lender, he may not pay the rent either.

You can solve this one big problem, but you must solve it carefully or you can become the victim. If you buy a house in foreclosure and then rent it back to the owners, there are three requirements:

1. Make sure that the sellers understand what they are doing. Because they are not moving, they may think that they are borrowing money, not selling their home. Be clear in what you say and specific in what you write down. Document clearly that this is a sale, not a loan. In a separate document, agree to rent the former owners the house.
2. Something has to change before renting to the sellers makes sense (either the house they are in or another rental you have). Has their income increased or their expenses decreased? How much rent can they afford to pay? They proved that they cannot afford the current house payments. How much can they afford?
3. Always build in a financial incentive for the sellers to pay the rent on time and then at some point to move out of the house and leave it in good condition. You want them to be able to afford the rent and then to leave you a house in good condition when they leave. They will be more likely to do these things if they are paid to do them. Build into your offer a reduced rent if they pay on time, and then more money when they move out, if they leave the house clean and in good repair.

Buying a House and Renting It Back To an Owner Who Is Behind on His Payments

Many homeowners who are behind on their payments like their house and don't want to move. Moving is expensive and not a lot of fun. You can buy a house using this strategy, but you must use a great deal of caution and common sense. Remember: If the homeowner is not making payments to the lender, you have to structure a deal that she can afford, or she won't make payments to you either.

Note: Some states have laws designed to protect sellers who are behind in their payments. These laws may address buying a house from a seller who is behind in his payments and then renting it back to him. Other states allow the seller to back out of the contract within a certain period of time. Understand your state laws that deal with foreclosures before entering into any agreement with a seller who is behind in their payments.

NEGOTIATING A PURCHASE AND LEASE

If the sellers have equity in their house, you can let them use that equity to pay rent on either their own house or another. For example, if their house is worth between $140,000 and $150,000 (always give yourself a range of prices) and their loan balance with back payments is $120,000, then they have about $20,000 equity that they could use to pay rent.

Market value of house in foreclosure:	$140,000–$150,000
Balance on loan (including back payments and costs):	$120,000
Their equity:	$20,000

The owners' payments today (that they *cannot* afford) with taxes and insurance are $1,250 a month.

During your initial conversation, ask the owners what their house would rent for. They often have a high opinion of what their house is worth and what it will rent for. If during your negotiation you determine that they want to stay in their house, you can then use their rent estimate as a starting point.

If they guessed low or you are uncertain of the market rent, then you need to gather comparable market rent information to establish a rent. In the preceding example of a house with a wholesale value of $140,000, the market rent may be between $1,200 and $1,400 a month.

Next, it is important to determine the amount of rent that the owners can comfortably afford to pay. Ask them what they can afford. Ask them how much income they have. They should pay around one-third of their income in rent. Do not rent them the house at a rent higher than one-third of their income.

Next, establish the amount of security deposit that gives them enough incentive to give you the house in good condition. The amount will depend on the value and condition of the house and the risk that you are taking by renting them the house.

Always make the deposit greater than a month's rent. If the house is in good condition, use several months' rent. Some states have laws that set a maximum security deposit. Learn your state law—it will be under the "Landlord-Tenant" heading in your state statutes.

By keeping the rent low and the deposit high, you give the owners a large financial incentive to stay in the house and to give it back in good condition. If they leave early, you can rent the house to another tenant for more rent.

Assume that the owners in this example had lost their jobs but have now found new, lower-paying, jobs. Their monthly income has dropped from $4,000 to $3,000. With this income, they can afford to pay about 33 percent, or about $1,000 a month in rent.

Their greatest problem is finding affordable housing until they can get back on their feet. Moving is expensive. If you let them rent back their own home, you have saved them a lot of hard work and expense, not to mention the trauma of moving from their nice home into a neighborhood that they can now afford.

Offer to rent them the house for one year at the bargain price of $900 a month, a $500 monthly discount from the high end of the market rent of $1,400. Understand, that $1,400 is high-retail rent. If you rented to another tenant today, you would be more likely to collect around $1,200 a month.

Fair market rent:	$1,200–$1,400
Rent to the previous owner:	$900
Monthly saving to them:	$300–$500

If you rent to them for 12 months at this $500 discount, they would save $6,000. In addition, you could give them a credit of $2,000 as the security deposit, which you would refund at the end of the 12 months if they turn over the house clean and in good condition. Giving this large a credit as a security deposit is important. You need to give them a significant incentive to keep the house in good condition, leave it clean, and leave on time.

Calculating the benefit of the lease to them is as follows:

Discounted rent (12 months × $500):	$6,000
Security deposit:	$2,000
Total benefit if they stay 12 months:	$8,000

If they want to extend the lease and continue living in the house as tenants, then you can raise the rent to closer to a market rate. I have rented back to sellers for as long as five years at a reduced rate. You can build in an increase each year.

Using the preceding house with a market rent of between $1,200 and $1,400 today, a five-year rent schedule could look like this:

Year one:	$ 900
Year two:	$1,000
Year three:	$1,100
Year four:	$1,200
Year five:	$1,300

By the time you reach the fifth year, you may be approaching market rent. Having a tenant stay in the house five years eliminates all vacancy costs, advertising costs, and a lot of maintenance expense. It can be a good deal for both you and the tenant. When you purchase a house using this technique, you often can make a deal that other buyers cannot make. You are offering a solution to the homeowners' biggest problem: where to live. In addition, you are saving them from a foreclosure.

Before you make the offer, calculate your potential profit, and make sure that the profit you will make will be fair for the amount of money and risk you are taking. In the preceding example, you are buying a house worth at least $140,000 for a total price of $126,200 (the loan balance of $120,000, the rent loss of $4,200, and the security deposit of $2,000). You may be able to buy this house with little or no down payment, depending on your ability to negotiate with the lender. If so, your risk is relatively low, and your profit potential when the former owners move out in a year should be a minimum of $13,800 and hopefully between $22,000 and $32,000.

Market value of house:	$140,000–$150,000
Existing loan balance:	$120,000
Loss on rent ($350 × 12 months):	$4,200 ($1,250 loan payments less $900 rent)
Security deposit:	$2,000
Total:	$126,200
Your purchase price:	$126,200
Potential profit:	$13,800–$23,800

WHEN NEGOTIATING WITH LENDERS, ASK FOR MORE THAN YOU EXPECT

Before you take title to a property, contact the lender. You need to talk with a high-ranking employee who has the authority to renegotiate the terms of the loan. This may be the president of a small bank, the senior mortgage officer of a midsized bank, or the person in charge of the department in a large bank that handles delinquent loans. You often can get the name and number of the appropriate person from correspondence sent to the homeowners by the lender after they fall behind in their payments.

You often will begin with a lower-level employee and have to ask to speak with the supervisor. Keep asking until you get to a decision maker.

Remember, you are dealing with employees in a big institution. It's not their money, but a bad loan is their problem. You can be the solution to that problem.

Once you are speaking to the right person, you need to have a plan. You can ask for many things that would benefit you, for example, a lower interest rate, a lower monthly payment, the forgiveness of the back payments and penalties (if not forgiveness, ask the person to add the amount of any delinquent payments to the loan), or a clause that will let you sell the house to a new buyer who can assume the loan without qualifying.

Ask for a lot. It will work in your favor because the lender will see you as a professional buyer, not an amateur.

If an institution owns the second mortgage or trust deed, see if it would be willing to lend you enough to pay off the first loan and add it to the second mortgage. That lender then would have a first mortgage in the amount of both the first and second mortgages.

Negotiate an interest rate that will allow you to make a profit. You may agree to a shorter-term loan, say, five years, to get a lower rate. If you need money to fix up or remodel the house, ask the lender to lend it to you and add it to the loan. If it's a great deal for you, but the lender is unwilling, offer to provide additional collateral. You could give the lender a second mortgage on another house that you own with equity.

BUYING FORECLOSURES TAKES KNOWLEDGE AND EXPERIENCE

There are a lot of highly skilled, professional foreclosure buyers. This group includes attorneys and others with knowledge of the system and the market. They are your competition. Buying foreclosures successfully requires experience, knowledge, and good legal advice.

In a rising interest-rate market, there are generally more foreclosures and a good deal of opportunity. Although tremendous opportunities are available, be careful not to buy beyond your ability to manage and handle the cash flow.

Let this be the beginning of your education because there is much more to learn. If you are a beginning investor, get good legal advice before bidding at a foreclosure sale or entering into a contract to buy a property from owners who are behind on their payments. The laws that govern the sale of foreclosures change. Check them before you buy.

13

ATTRACTING AND TRAINING LONG-TERM, LOW-MAINTENANCE TENANTS

What qualities are you looking for in a good tenant? When I ask investors in my seminar this question, here are the responses I get:

1. A tenant who pays on time
2. A tenant who takes care of the property
3. A tenant who stays forever
4. A tenants who never calls

Now turn the question around. What is a good tenant (one who will do the preceding) looking for in a house and in a landlord? You probably have rented a house or an apartment. What was important to you as a renter? Here is a partial list of what good tenants tell me they are looking for:

1. A house in a safe neighborhood
2. A house big enough to hold all our stuff
3. A house that is clean and in good repair

4. A landlord who will maintain the property
5. Fair rent
6. Fair rent raises
7. Privacy
8. A house that is not for sale

Is there anything on this list that you would find difficult to provide?

THE SECRET OF GETTING THE BEST TENANTS IN YOUR TOWN

The best tenants have their choice of houses to rent because every landlord with a vacancy would love to meet them. You can attract the best tenants in your town. The secret is simple. Most of the features listed below were covered in Chapter 2. This is no accident: The right house will attract a superior tenant.

First, buy a well-designed house in a good neighborhood. Good neighbors are what everyone wants, and tenants are no exception. If the neighbors on both sides and across the street take good care of their property and are good neighbors, then you can attract a tenant who values a good neighbor.

Avoid neighborhoods full of tenants. Most landlords do not maintain property well or manage tenants well, so you can spot the tenant-occupied houses. Buy in owner-occupied neighborhoods, and then keep your house looking as good as the neighbors' houses.

Avoid strange houses. Some people design and build their own homes, and some of these people are not good at it. Houses that are unique will appeal only to unique people. You will see houses that have strange floor plans or exteriors. Other houses have been remodeled poorly, so you have to walk through one bedroom to get to another bedroom. These houses are hard to rent and hard to sell. There is a house in our town that is built to resemble a ship, with a lighthouse and all. Few people actually want to live in a house that looks like a boat. Use your common sense to avoid houses that are not normal. You can buy them cheap, but in the long run, you will make less money.

Avoid houses on busy streets and on corner lots. Corner lots often have little or no back yard, and busy streets are noisy and dangerous.

Buy the best location you can afford. The best-located houses will appreciate the most and be the easiest to rent.

BUY A HOUSE WITH ROOM FOR LOTS OF STUFF

Next, buy a house that is big enough for a family of four or five people to live in comfortably. Smaller families still appreciate the extra space, and it gives them room for guests or "new additions."

Houses with three bedrooms and two bathrooms are more rentable than a smaller home, and a garage or basement for storage is a must-have feature. You want to rent to a tenant who owns a bunch of stuff and does not find moving fun. One reason that house tenants tend to stay in one place much longer than apartment tenants is that they have more stuff. The more stuff you have to move, the less likely you are to move.

A yard that is fenced or that can be fenced is a great asset. Most of my tenants have kids or pets or both. One reason they need a house instead of an apartment is the kids and pets. The kids and pets also will keep them cash poor, so it increases the chances that they will stay a long time.

UNDERSTANDING THE LAWS THAT APPLY TO LANDLORDING

There are local, state, and federal laws that affect you as a landlord. Your local laws, such as zoning regulations, determine what you can do with a property. A house zoned single-family residential may not be used to house a business. Other local laws may require you to maintain your property. Local code-enforcement departments generally enforce these laws.

Your state has laws that regulate the relationships between landlords and tenants. Get a copy of your state's landlord-tenant statute that applies to single-family rentals. Your state statutes will be available in your public library, and now they often are available online. It is almost certain that there are separate statute sections that apply to multifamily, mobile home, and commercial rentals.

Read the part of the law that deals with single-family tenancies carefully. Learn what maintenance you are required to provide and what your tenant is required to do. Know how large a security deposit you can charge, where you have to hold it, and how you handle the return of the deposit when a tenant moves out of the house.

Learn what steps you need to take if a tenant refuses to pay you rent. Hopefully, you will not use this information often. In 33 years of managing hundreds of tenants, I have had to evict only six tenants.

Many more tenants have had problems, but by quickly addressing those problems, I avoided using the court system to evict. If you have a problem with a tenant, your recourse will be in your local courts, and the process is guided by your state statutes. By understanding and complying with your state statutes, you can avoid going to court, except in cases where the tenants refuse to negotiate.

Federal fair housing (antidiscrimination) laws apply to renting and selling houses. A copy can be found online by searching for The Fair Housing Act or, again, in your public library. Read the Fair Housing Act to learn how it affects you as a residential landlord. It prohibits discrimination in the sale or rental of a house based on race, color, religion, sex, familial status, or national origin and explains your obligations if you rent to someone with a significant handicap.

THE STEPS IN RENTING A HOUSE

Here are the steps that you take to attract, select, and rent to a good tenant.

1. Get the Property Clean and in Good Repair

Always get a house in good condition before you rent it. It's a mistake to rent a dirty house or one that needs work. When you do, you will probably get a dirty tenant who will leave you with an even dirtier house that needs even more work. Tenants may promise to do work or clean, but they rarely do it.

How much does it cost to have a house professionally cleaned in your town? Typically it is the equivalent of only a few days rent. Who makes the decision to rent a house? If you rent to a couple, the woman typically will be the decision maker, and women prefer a clean house (because they know who will have to clean it).

Spend the money to clean the whole house: windows, screens, closets, and cabinets. Touch up or paint the house as needed. Spruce up the yard, and make sure that the house looks good from the street. A house may be beautiful inside, but if it's a dog from the street, no one is going to stop to look in the windows.

If a house rents for $1,000 a month, it costs you about $33 a day to let it sit empty. In addition, you probably are running a $300 a month ad and taking the time to keep the grass cut and answer the phone.

Anticipate vacancies, and move fast to clean them and spruce them up. If you can rent a house in a week instead of a month because you paid a housecleaner and a painter a little extra to work over the weekend, you are way ahead of the person who takes several weeks to paint and clean the house himself.

2. Introduce Yourself to the Neighbors

Knowing the neighbors keeps out bad tenants. When I buy a house that I intend to rent, I always introduce myself to the neighbors and give them my name and phone number. I tell them that if a tenant causes them any kind of problem, I want to hear from them and that I will do everything I can to take care of it. I want my tenants to be good neighbors, and I want good neighbors that are there to stay.

I then tell my prospective tenants that I know the neighbors and that they keep an eye on the house for me. A prospective tenant who was planning on sneaking several more roommates in or using the house for a business or even illegal purpose will not want to rent a house that is so well monitored. Such a person will leave and rent a different house.

3. Set the Rent and the Deposit

Before you begin to rent a house, write down the rent, the deposit, and the amount of income that a tenant would need to afford your house. Typically, a tenant can afford to pay between 30 and 40 percent of her income as rent. Many tenants will want to rent a house that they cannot afford. It is up to you to use good judgment and not allow potential tenants to obligate themselves to too much rent.

Setting the rent and deposit is not an exact science, and you can give yourself a range rather than an absolute number for a tenant's income. Charge a security deposit that is an amount greater than a month's rent.

If it is the same as a month's rent, tenants will assume that they can use it to pay the last month's rent. The only money that helps you as a landlord is money you have left after the tenant moves out. The bigger the security deposit you have, the more the tenant will want it back, and the more cooperative that tenant will be.

Research your state tenant and landlord laws to see if there are restrictions on the amount of the security deposit you can charge. Most states allow a deposit of at least a month and a half's rent, and many allow two months' rent.

While you are better off with the biggest deposit you can charge, tenants will only pay so much. They will pay a larger deposit to get a better house at a fair rent. A bigger deposit will eliminate many financially marginal tenants. By charging a larger deposit, at least a month and a half's rent, you can rent to a tenant who is financially stronger and is smart enough to pay a little higher deposit to get a better house.

Monthly Rent	Tenants' Monthly Income Range	Security Deposit
$500	$1,250–$1,666	$750–$1,000
$750	$1,875–$2,500	$1,125–$1,500
$1,000	$2,500–$3,333	$1,500–$2,000
$1,500	$3,750–$5,000	$2,250–$3,000

Look at both the quantity and quality of the income. Some tenants make too much money to rent your house. They can afford it easily, but they also can afford to buy, and typically, they will and will stay only a short time.

A tenant with a new job or working in a new field is a much higher risk than a tenant with a longer-term job. A tenant on commission is a higher risk than one paid by the hour or on salary. Ask potential tenants where they work and how long they have worked there. Ask for both their income and their immediate supervisor's name and phone number.

4. When the Rental Market Is Soft, Lower Your Rent, Not Your Standards

When the rental market is soft (there are many houses for rent and not many qualified tenants to rent them), rather than lowering your standards, reduce your rent to attract a quality tenant who recognizes a bargain. There are always some good tenants looking for a house. To attract them, you need a good house in a good neighborhood that is attractively priced. When you calculate the cost of letting your house sit empty for a month, it is far better strategy to price your house on the low side of the market to begin with and to attract the best available tenant immediately rather than pricing it higher and waiting longer for a qualified tenant.

If a house rents for $1,200 a month and sits empty for a month before you rent it, it costs you $1,200 plus the cost of advertising and maintaining the house. Renting it the first week at $1,100 a month will make you more money and take less of your time. When you have an empty house, in addition to advertising and maintaining it, you have to answer the phone and interview prospective tenants. This takes a lot of your time. Otherwise, you could use the time to find another good deal.

Try to reduce your rent, not your deposit. Although they move together, you don't want to rent to someone who cannot afford your house. The best test of this is whether the potential tenants have money in the bank today.

5. Place an Ad in the Paper (Make Sure to Include the Amount of the Rent)

Classified advertising is expensive. You may have more than one paper that you could use to advertise you properties. Use a short ad, but make these important points: the price, the location, the size, the condition, and who you will accept. The price is important because research shows that people do not call on unpriced ads. Here is a typical ad:

Available Immediately, 3/2/2

$1,100 monthly. Clean, new tile and carpet.

Kids, pets OK. 366-9024

Some papers arrange the ads alphabetically. If so, be creative and use a first word that starts with *A*.

6. Place a Sign on the Property

Use a good-looking sign with your phone number in larger numbers. Put an information sheet showing the price and features of the house in a front window. Leave the blinds and drapes open so that prospective tenants can see the interior.

7. Notify the Neighbors

Send the neighbors a short letter or postcard and tell them the rent amount in case they have friends looking for a place to live.

8. Arrange for Lawn Care During Vacancy

Keep the outside looking good. Try to use a neighborhood kid or local service to mow, and the worker(s) also will keep an eye on the house for you.

9. Make Sure Your Phone Is Answered

Some landlords use a dedicated cellphone for calls on ads. If you cannot answer it, put recorded information about the house and about how prospective tenants can contact you, either during office hours or at an open house that you have scheduled.

10. Showing the Property

Rather than meeting prospective tenants at the house, tell them to drive by the house, look in the windows if it is vacant, and then to give you a call back if they want to see the inside. If they have seen the outside and want the house, ask them to meet you to fill out an application and to leave a deposit (I currently ask for a $100 deposit that I will refund if I don't rent to them or that I will apply to the rent if I do rent to them). After you have met them and they have filled out an application and you like them, then you can meet them at the house or give them a key to the house to inspect it. If you give them a key, have them sign a receipt that says, "We agree not to occupy the house, to lock the house when we leave, that no one will smoke in the property, and that we turn off any lights, water, etc., before leaving and that we will return the key within ____ hours, and we are responsible for any damage to the house." Don't worry about theft. If someone is going to steal something out of your house, they are not going to fill out an application first; they will just break into the house.

11. Holding Open Houses

An alternative is to hold an open house at the rental house at a certain time and invite all who are interested to meet you there. Pick a time that will work for most tenants. Between 4:30 and 6 P.M. is a good time for most. You can do this once a week or more often depending on the number of calls you get and how eager you are to rent the house. Put a note in the window of the house with the time and date. Bring applications and rental agreements with you. Come prepared to rent the house.

12. Have the Prospective Tenant Fill Out an Application

Once prospective tenants have seen a house and want it, have them fill out a rental application. Check with your local investor's association or apartment owner's association for locally used forms and rental contracts. Another source may be a local real estate attorney who hands out free forms to drum up business. Many forms are available online. (Professional Publishers has both applications and residential rental contracts at a reasonable cost.)

If your application does not ask how long the prospective tenants intend to stay, you ask it, without giving them clues to the answer that you want. The right answer is "the rest of our lives," but most tenants say one or two years. Obviously, two years is a better answer; I want people who will unpack and stay a while. The longer they stay, the more money they make me.

Ask prospective tenants for an application fee with their application. I ask for $100, which I refund if I refuse to rent them the house or apply to the security deposit if I rent to them. State laws vary on how much you can charge for application fees and security deposits. Get a copy of your state landlord-tenant statute and really become knowledgeable about the sections that deal with residential leases.

13. Check Their References

Call the prospective tenants' employer(s) to confirm employment and income, and call their current and immediate past landlords to ask whether they would rent to these tenants again. To make sure that you are really talking to the right person, confirm the facts that the tenants gave you. For example, the tenants may have stated that they had paid $1,000 a month rent and had lived in the previous property three years. Ask the landlord the amount of rent and how long the tenants have lived there. If it's just a friend of the tenant instead of the landlord, he may not know the answers.

14. Interview the Tenants

Before you agree to rent someone a house, you want to spend some time with them and interview them. You want them to see you as a competent landlord who has rules and wants to rent his house to tenants who will take care of the house and be good neighbors.

Part of the interview is just getting to know them. Ask where they are from, where they went to school, how many kids they have, where their family lives, what activities their kids are involved in, why they like this house and this neighborhood, and so on.

Invite the entire family to the interview so that you can see how the parents interact with the kids. Jack Miller, a very successful landlord, says that he watches out for the "fake kid." A fake kid is one who is dressed too well or behaves too well. Normal kids squirm and want the parents' attention. The way in which the parents handle a real kid shows you how the family interacts.

Always ask the kids, not the parents, what pets they have. Sometimes parents forget to list the pets on the application. The kids will tell you all about their pets.

This "small talk" will allow you to get to learn much more than the prospective tenants listed on the application. You want to rent to real people who can answer these normal questions comfortably.

When you are interviewing potential tenants, ask them if they have had any credit problems. Most tenants will tell you if they do because they assume that you are going to check.

Some new landlords are looking for the perfect tenant. Call other landlords in your town, and you will find some who want a tenant without kids or pets, a nonsmoking, nondrinker, with a steady job, and good credit.

Such tenants may be out there looking for a house, but they are few and far between. Most of my tenants have both kids and pets, and many have some credit problems. I like tenants with all three because they stay longer. They need me more than I need them. With a little training, they can become great tenants.

There are many honest, hardworking tenants looking for houses, but they are not perfect. Look for ones that can look you in the eye and answer your direct questions. Watch for body language and how the spouse and kids react. Normal couples will both have questions. Questions are a good sign. Tenants who have no questions and are anxious to sign are desperate for a house. Keep talking to them until you find out why. If you don't like the reason, don't rent to them.

Look for signs of stability, such as staying a long time on a job or several years with a previous landlord. Ask why they are moving. If their reason is that their current landlord won't fix anything, you might wonder why so many things needed fixing. Dig in and ask more questions about what needed fixing and why.

Avoid tenants who need a place tonight. Perhaps they have to move today because they were evicted. Normal people plan ahead more than one day.

15. Collect a Cash Deposit or a Cashier's Check Made Out to You

In William Nickerson's classic book on real estate investing, *How I Turned $10,000 into $1,000,000 in My Spare Time,* he advised to never accept anything but cash for a security deposit. Nickerson was a hands-on landlord, and his book is still a must-read for investors.

Always get your houses in good shape before you rent them, and then always require cash or a cashier's check with a current date drawn on a local bank for the deposit. (You can stop payment on a cashier's check—beware of ones with old dates.) If you make the mistake of letting tenants move in and take a bad check for the rent and deposit, you will have to evict to get them out. That will take you a month or more. Because they did this intentionally (and fraudulently), they are unlikely to return your house clean and in good condition.

Tenants are creative and want you to accept something other than money for the deposit. Tenants with no money will try to talk you into renting them a house. Their pitch is that "they will take the house in its current deplorable condition [it's actually in good shape] and do all the work it needs instead of paying a deposit or first month's rent." Recognize this technique, and don't accept a story in the place of money.

16. Give the Keys, a Copy of the Rental Agreement, and an Inspection Sheet to Tenants Only After the Full Deposit and Rent Have Been Paid

Do not let tenants begin to move in until they have paid you all that they owe you.

17. Cancel the Ad and Remove the Sign

If you have more than one house for rent, callers from one sign can rent the other house. You may decide to leave the sign up until the tenants move in to generate more calls.

18. Note the Return—or Lack Thereof—of the Inspection Sheet

Always require new tenants to fill out and return to you an inspection sheet that shows the condition of the house the day they moved in. Give them only a few days to return this to you, and explain that if they fail to return it, they are stating that the house is in good condition. If there is something that needs attention, get it fixed as soon as possible.

19. Note the Deposit Amount and Rent Amount on a Bookkeeping Sheet

Circle the deposit in red so that you do not accidentally include it in your income. The security deposit is not taxable income but can be reported accidentally that way unless you are careful to note it. Learn your state laws that govern how you must handle security deposits. Some states require you to hold them in a separate account.

20. Note the Rental Amount and Due Date on Your Monthly Checklist

Have a paper checklist that lists your properties by tenants, rental amount, and due date. Have your rents all come due on the same day of the month. Most use the first because it is easier for tenants to remember. When you rent a house, prorate the first month's rent to have it fall due on the first day of the next month. If the tenants are moving in the last half of the month, collect a full month's rent and then prorate the next month's rent.

21. Have a System to Remind You When the Agreement Expires

Then plan to renew and evaluate the monthly rent prior to the expiration date.

SELECTING THE RIGHT TENANTS

After reading the Fair Housing Act, make your rules for selecting tenants comply with the federal rules. As a landlord, you can still have standards. You just need to apply those standards equally to everyone.

What is really important to you as a landlord? If you agree with my list, the top three qualities are (1) you want someone who will pay the rent on time, (2) will take care of the property, and (3) will stay "forever." You can select your tenants based on both their history of accomplishing these actions and their potential for future performance on these important issues.

You can refuse to rent to a tenant who cannot afford your house. Before you begin the process of renting a house, set the rent and deposit amount, and tell every person who calls the same information. Not renting to someone who cannot afford your house is not discrimination; it is good business. You simply need to treat all applicants equally.

Likewise, if you require that a tenant have a certain level of income to rent your house, write down how much that will be for this house, and again, treat everyone equally. You can require proof of income, but do it for everyone.

Gross income is not the only consideration. The debt or other obligations potential tenants have, such as car or furniture payments, affect their ability to pay. The number of children and other dependents they have or other extraordinary expenses, such as a hospital debt they are obligated to repay, make them a higher-risk tenant.

Many potential tenants have some credit problems. These problems may be preventing them from buying a house. Some credit problems are a result of a catastrophe, such as a divorce, an automobile accident, or a business failure. If the prospective tenants are recovering and are able to pay their current bills, then they may be good risks as tenants. Most tenants have had some financial problems, or they would not be tenants.

You can refuse to rent to tenants who are abusing their current residence because they likely will abuse yours. The way tenants maintain their car is also an indication of how they will maintain your house. Look at their car, and if possible, go inspect the house in which they live. You want to rent to responsible tenants who will maintain your house. You can require them to do this with your agreement, but if they are unwilling or incapable of taking care of your house, you don't want to rent to them.

Third, you are looking for tenants with long-term potential. My average tenant stays five years or more. If they stay at least two years, they have made me a profit. Tenants who move out in a year cost me money. It is expensive to have tenants move out and replace them with another. It may cost you thousands of dollars depending on how long it takes you to find a replacement tenant. Although you never really know how long someone will stay, you can look for signs of potential stability.

Ask these questions on your application: How long have you lived in your current residence? How long did you live in your previous residence? What were the addresses? (If they can't remember the addresses, they weren't there very long.)

Ask for the current and previous landlords' names and phone numbers. Often the previous landlord may be a better source of information than a current landlord who may be happy for them to move. Call the previous landlord and ask one simple question: "Would you rent to these tenants again?" If the landlord says no, ask why.

Job stability and the type of job prospective tenants have are additional clues to potential longevity. If they are transferred often, they are a higher risk. Local family connections are another good sign.

RENTING TO YOUR FIRST TENANT

The first time you rent a house, you are likely to be confused about how to screen and select tenants. When tenants call on your ad, tell them the amount of the rent and the deposit. Some will ask if they can pay over time, and others will tell you that you are charging too much. Neither of these tenants has the money to move into your house.

You are better off with an empty house than with a house occupied by tenants who cannot afford to pay the rent. Set standards, and stick with them.

Ask everyone for proof of income. If a tenant is a salesman or self-employed, require two years' tax returns. Make sure that they are signed copies of the original. Call references and confirm income if the tenant is employed.

Just before you conduct your interview, go back and review this section, and write down your requirements for a tenant for this house.

Most new landlords are concerned about how they can turn down tenants they don't want to rent to. Turn them down because of a business reason, not a personal reason. Here are some business reasons you can use to turn down a tenant who does not qualify to rent your house:

1. They will not fill out an application.
2. They will not give you an application fee.
3. They do not have enough money for the first month's rent and the security deposit.
4. They do not make enough money to afford the rent.
5. They do not have a verifiable source of income.
6. They do not have a steady record of employment.
7. They do not have a good history as a tenant.
8. They cannot give you a referral that you can contact.
9. They do not plan to stay as long as you want a tenant to stay.
10. They have a big dog (or several dogs or cats—or any animals you don't like—animals are not a protected class).
11. They have too many vehicles or a large truck or motor home.

This is not an all-inclusive list, but it will give you an idea of the types of reasons you can use to turn down a tenant.

In summary, you want to rent to a tenant who has a verifiable source of income that is large enough to afford your house. A tenant with long-term potential is preferable to a better-looking tenant who likely will move in six months. A tenant who moves in less than two years is costing you money. Set your goal to have your average tenant stay at least three years, and you will be a happy and successful landlord.

REWARDING YOUR GOOD TENANTS WITH FINANCIAL INCENTIVES

In my first years of renting houses, another landlord shared a technique that he used in Philadelphia during the 1940s to collect rent on time. Rather than charging a late penalty like most landlords, he gave his tenants a discount for paying on or before the first of the month. The amount of the discount was meaningful enough that his tenants paid him first. If they were short that month, they paid someone else late.

The concept of giving a good tenant a real discount to pay on time works well. Today, I combine the discount for on-time payment with a discount for not calling for maintenance that month. As a tenant, you have to do both—pay on time and not call for maintenance—to earn your discount.

With this approach, tenants may just defer maintenance for months or even years. To use this discount approach safely, you also must collect a substantial security deposit and inspect your homes periodically. Your rental contract should include a clause that says any deferred maintenance that is the responsibility of the tenants will be charged against the security deposit when the tenants move out of the property.

The concept of giving a financial incentive works so well with good tenants that you rarely see them. Some of my tenants have been with me for more than 20 years—really. And during that time they have paid on time every month. These tenants are making me a lot of money and, just as important, not taking any of my time.

Other ways to reward exemplary tenants is for you to agree to pay for improvements or additions to the house that benefit the tenant. Fencing in a yard, screening a porch, adding landscaping, paying for the materials to build a deck or a fence, or simply allowing the tenant to make some modifications to the house, such as wallpaper or a different color paint, bond the tenant to your house.

My tenants have recarpeted, painted, replaced and refinished cabinets, and installed decks and patios, all at their own expense. My longest-term tenants moved into a new house I had built 26 years ago and plan on living there for as long as they can.

Not every tenant will be a great tenant, but when you get one, take good care of him with reasonable rent raises and prompt responses to normal maintenance problems. Long-term tenants are worth tens of thousands of dollars to you because they keep you from having vacancies and keep your repair bills lower. You will spend most of your money as a landlord when you have tenant turnover. Do what you can to minimize it.

BEING A SUCCESSFUL LANDLORD, WITHOUT WORKING NIGHTS OR WEEKENDS

Many people avoid buying real estate because they fear getting a phone call from a tenant in the middle of the night. In more than 30 years as a landlord, I have never taken a tenant's call at home. Early on I decided to work no more than my banker, and he does not work nights or weekends. You can be a success as a landlord and work no harder than your banker.

In the rare event of an actual emergency, you can furnish your tenants with a list of numbers for emergency contacts. I have had five actual emergencies in about 30 years of managing hundreds of tenants: two fires (solution: call 911), two break-ins (solution: call the police), and a broken pipe causing a flood (solution: call the plumber).

Not everything that a tenant would see as an emergency is an emergency to me. For example, several years ago on Thanksgiving morning one of my tenants could not get her oven to work. She thought it was an emergency, called my office number, and left an emergency message with the answering service. But I did not respond until the following Monday, at which time the urgency was long forgotten. If I had called her Thanksgiving morning, she would have been upset with me if I did not offer to find a repairman to fix her oven. It would have been nearly impossible—and very expensive—to find a repairman who would make a house call on Thanksgiving morning.

By the time I called her on the Monday morning after Thanksgiving, she had forgotten why she had called. The moment had passed. The emergency was over, and we could deal with the minor repair rationally, not emotionally.

Most "emergencies," like a hot water heater not heating, an air conditioner that is not cooling properly, or a drain line that is plugged, are not real emergencies and can be handled during business hours.

Real emergencies include fires, a tree falling on a roof and creating a leak, a plumbing problem flooding the house, an electrical problem that is dangerous, a break-in where the house cannot be secured, and other problems that may result in injury to tenants or others.

You can delegate to tenants the responsibility for clogged drain lines (which they clogged), damaged screens or broken windows (which they damaged or broke), and anything else that they break. You can have them coordinate the repair of almost anything else—after you authorize it.

A couple of years ago I came to work on Monday morning, and a neighbor had called and left a message that the police had raided one of my houses and kicked in the front door. I tried calling the tenant and got no response, so I drove out to see the house. By the time I arrived, the tenant had purchased and installed a new front door to replace the one the police had damaged. It turns out that he had a problem that warranted the police arresting him, but he made bail, fixed the door, and lived there for many months until the judge made him an offer he could not refuse.

Although the tenant was in trouble with the authorities, he valued his home and wanted to continue living in it. I had treated him fairly and had provided him a good place to live at a fair price. He knew that he had an obligation to fix things that he damaged, so he fixed the front door and continued to pay the rent until he moved.

BEING FIRM AND FAIR WITH TENANTS WHO TEST YOU

Tenants will test your system. If you give them a discount for paying by the first of the month, they will bring the discounted amount in (or mail it in) so that you receive it on the second. If you accept it and still let them take the discount, the next month it will come on the fifth and then the tenth, and so on. If you give someone a financial incentive for good behavior, don't reward bad behavior. Be nice, but smile like your banker would smile if you tried to talk him out of a late charge on your monthly payment. Tell such tenants that you hope that they pay on time next month so that they can qualify for the discount. Collect the full rent, or you are training them to pay late.

MOVE-IN AND MOVE-OUT INSPECTIONS

Likewise, tenants will test you and ask you to do repairs that are their responsibility. When they do, be fair but firm. When tenants move into a house, I give them a detailed inspection sheet, which I ask them to fill out and return to me within three days of taking occupancy. I want it back quickly so that I have an accurate record of the condition of the house. I already have on file the previous tenants' sheet, and now I can compare them. The new tenants are doing the exit inspection for the old tenants, and they will be thorough.

After the three-day period, I hold the tenants accountable for any damage to the property. If they plug up the plumbing or break something, it is their responsibility to handle the maintenance call and repair on their own without involving me. If they do involve me, they will lose their discount and still may be responsible for the repair if they are at fault.

CONSISTENCY AND CONTROL—THE KEYS TO EFFECTIVE MANAGEMENT

A good property manager does not have to think a lot. He just needs to have a good set of policies and procedures and then follow them. If you find yourself making up a new answer for every tenant question, then you need to think through your policies, write them down, and be consistent with all your tenants.

Landlords get in trouble when they treat tenants differently. Establish policies, and then stick with them.

The secret to being a happy, successful landlord can be summed up in a word—*control.* Many people who invest in real estate do it because they like to be in control of their investments. Landlords who are miserable have lost control. Their tenants are running the show.

TRAINING YOUR TENANTS

Either you will train your tenants, or they will train you. I use the word *train* here not as in training a pet simply to respond to a command. Rather, tenants will learn what they can expect from you, when you respond to their requests, or when they test your system of management.

Attracting and Training Long-Term, Low-Maintenance Tenants

Good tenants are looking for fair and responsive landlords. Being fair and responsive will not necessarily cost you money. In fact, if prospective tenants believe that you are both fair and responsive, they are more likely to rent from you. Many landlords are neither.

To be in control as a landlord, you need a management system that both you and your tenants understand and that you implement. Like teenagers, tenants will search for boundaries and then test them. As the landlord, you need to set those boundaries clearly. When you are tested, restate the boundaries and be fair but firm in sticking with the rules.

Training starts with your first contact with prospective tenants and continues through your entire relationship with them. You set the stage with your rental application and initial interview. After that, your response to requests will train people to call more often or to handle their own problems.

It is important that you have policies, that your policies comply with the law, and that you enforce those policies. In more than 30 years of managing hundreds of tenants and studying other successful landlords, I have established the following rules as policy for renting houses. Use them, and they will save you thousands of dollars and many hours of aggravation.

Single-Family House Management Policies

1. Always get cash (or a local cashier's check or money order) for the first month's rent and the security deposit. (Never accept an old or out-of-town cashier's check—they may have stopped payment on it.)
2. Never accept a partial security deposit and allow a tenant to have possession of the house. Prorate the rent, and take a full deposit. (You cannot evict for nonpayment of deposit.)
3. Always use an all-inclusive rental agreement with which you are comfortable and understand fully. Never negotiate the agreement with tenants. If they win this negotiation, they will negotiate more.
4. Always take the time to go over the entire agreement with all adults who will be living in the house. Try to interview the entire family.
5. Never discriminate. Treat every tenant and applicant equally and fairly. Do not bend policies because a tenant belongs to a minority. Treat *everyone* the same.

6. Have a late payment policy, and stick with it. When you make an exception, the exception will soon become the rule.
7. Always serve late tenants with notices as soon as they are late.
8. Feeling sorry for tenants doesn't help them or you. Pay them to move out; take action! Do not confuse business with charity, or you may not have the money to be charitable.
9. Keep good records of all income and receipts. Always give receipts for rent collected in cash; keep duplicate copies in a receipt book.
10. Respond to tenant requests in a reasonable and businesslike manner. Distinguish between ordinary maintenance and real emergencies. Have a system in place to handle true emergencies.
11. Keep the property in good repair, and inspect the outside of a property several times a year to ensure that tenants are taking care of the property.*

GETTING RID OF BAD TENANTS

The primary reason to move tenants out of a property before the term is up is that they are not paying rent. Take immediate action when tenants do not pay on time. Deliver to them a three-day pay or quit (move) notice. It is the first step in the eviction process. Read your state's statutes so that you know in advance what actions you need to take.

When tenants receive this prompt response to their nonpayment, typically they will pay you. If they don't pay you, the next step is to talk with them, if possible, to see if you can work out a payment schedule that they can afford.

Sometimes, converting tenants to a weekly pay schedule (at a higher rent) will make it possible for them to stay in the house. Take the monthly rent and divide it by four, and have the tenants begin to pay you this new amount every Friday. Since there are 52 Fridays in a year (not $4 \times 12 = 48$), you will receive an extra four weeks' rent each year for your trouble.

If this solution does not solve the problem, offer to return a portion of the security deposit if they move immediately. You can make the offer

*Reprinted from John Schaub's "Making It Big on Little Deals Seminar," 2004 by permission of Pro Serve Corporation of Sarasota, Inc.

this way: "I can hire an attorney to evict you, in which case you will lose your entire deposit, or I can give you part of your deposit back if you will move out by next Friday. Would you rather I pay you or an attorney?"

You must make this offer short term so that if they do not move as agreed, you still have enough deposit to protect you if you have to continue on with the eviction process. It's worth repeating myself and saying that I have had only six evictions in over 30 years of managing hundreds of tenants. The secret of having few evictions is a good selection process, following with an immediate response when a tenant does not pay. An eviction is the most expensive way to move a tenant out.

RAISING YOUR RENTS

You don't keep your tenants long term by not raising your rents. That would be an expensive tradeoff. To the contrary, raising your rents a little bit every year is good for you and your tenants. Your costs will go up most years. Your tenants expect some increase—the secret of keeping your tenants long term is a series of small increases.

Consider how a good tenant would react if you did not raise his rent for five years and then one year you jumped it $75 a month. The $75 a month increase may not catch him up to market rent, but it still will be a shock to him, and he may move. This would cost you a good tenant and the tenant a good home.

It would be better for you and the tenant to raise his rent $20 every year. Most tenants won't move to avoid a $20 increase in rent. It costs far more than that to move, not to mention the aggravation of moving.

Track your tenants, and raise their rents a moderate amount once a year. If there is a season of the year that tenants hate to move, time your rent increases to fall in that season, and fewer will move.

Even if you have several houses, raise your rents one house at a time. If you raise the rent and a tenant moves, you will want to assess the rental market carefully before you raise the rent for the next tenant.

If the rental market is soft and you want to keep your good tenants, put a handwritten note on the rent increase letter to call you if they have any questions. If they call and say that they will have to move if you raise the rent, you may decide to leave the rent alone this year to keep a good tenant.

During the three recessions I have weathered, I have lowered my rents to keep my good tenants. I'd rather be 100 percent full at 90 percent of market rent than 10 percent empty trying to get 100 percent of market rent.

When your houses are full of solid tenants, you can spend your time looking for good deals rather than trying to rent houses. A landlord who tries to squeeze the top dollar in rent out of a lot of his houses will spend a lot of time looking for new tenants.

Set your rents slightly below the market, charge a larger-than-average security deposit, keep your houses in good shape, and you can attract the best tenants in your town.

AVOIDING LANDLORD BURNOUT

Some landlords enjoy owning property all their life. In fact, owning and managing property is something you can do as long as you want to. Many of my more senior students are well into their eighties and still enjoy managing their money and their property. In doing the research for a book I coauthored entitled, *Optimal Aging,* (available at www.OptimalAging.com) I found that staying active in managing your financial affairs keeps you young and that you often will make better decisions than those to whom you delegate.

Other landlords suffer "burnout" and sell their property before they benefit from long-term appreciation and debt payoff.

There are a couple of keys to avoiding landlord burnout. The first is buying property that attracts long-term tenants who have the same value system that you do. You want to rent to tenants who see themselves as homeowners one day. These tenants will value the house they live in, and they may want a reference from you to either buy a house or to rent another.

There are big differences in how people view themselves and others. If you rent to people who are constantly trying to beat you out of the rent, eventually you will wear out.

Another key is avoiding high-turnover, high-management property. Renting low-income property to tenants who can't afford anything better is a hard way to make a fortune. People who live on the edge of financial disaster are high-management tenants. They often cannot pay the rent for real reasons.

The third key is to buy the right number of properties for you. Set your goals in terms of cash flow and net worth, not in term of numbers of properties. You may decide that you only need a few properties. Fewer properties mean fewer tenants and less work.

14

KNOWING WHEN TO SELL AND HOW TO SELL

Although my advice to investors for years has been to buy good property and then hold it forever, no book on investing in real estate would be complete without a chapter on selling. You will, as I have, buy some property that you don't want to keep. You will have other property that can be sold for large profits. Before you sell, ask yourself what you will do with the money. Ask yourself, what is your investment goal?

If your answer is to spend the profits on something good or fun or both, go for it—as long as it does not sabotage your investment plan. Suppose that your plan is to buy two houses a year for 10 years and then sell off enough property at the end of the 10 years to own 10 houses free and clear.

If you are ahead of your goal, selling a house to take a great vacation or to buy a larger home will not keep you from making your goal. Reward yourself and your family along the way so that they can see some short-term benefits of investing.

If you are considering making a significant gift to a church or charity, donating a house in which you have a large gain is a very efficient way to make a gift, without writing a check. You can give away your profit in the house, and take a charitable deduction against other income. Check with your tax advisor before you make the gift to get good advice on the best time and way to do it.

If you are going to sell and invest in something else, have it lined up before you sell. A real estate investor can reinvest the money from a sale into another investment without paying taxes under Section 1031 of the Internal Revenue Code. This is commonly called a *tax-deferred exchange* and is used widely by investors.

Jack Reed's excellent book, *Aggressive Tax Avoidance for Real Estate Investors* (www.johntreed.com), is a great short course on tax-deferred exchanges and installment sales and is a must-read for real estate investors. In addition to not paying taxes, an exchange forces you to reinvest your profits into another property. This keeps you from spending it on toys, which I am prone to do.

There are other investments that can be complementary to investing in houses. Notes secured by mortgages or trust deeds can provide higher short-term income than a house, but notes are not appreciating assets. To the contrary, if you sell a house and carry back a 10-year amortizing note, in 10 years, all the income will be history. If there is inflation, your payments will buy less with each succeeding year. While a house held for 10 years could double in value, the note value would go to zero. Note investing is much higher risk than real estate investing. Learn to make money with houses first, and then learn to make money with notes.

TEACH A MAN TO FISH AND NEXT WEEK HE'LL BE SHOPPING FOR A BOAT

A benefit of investing successfully is enjoying the money you make. A toy such as a boat, a plane, a vacation home, or even the house you live in can be a big drain on your finances. Such things also can be a tremendous motivator.

If you need a little push to get going, find a picture of something that you would really like to have—a new car or a vacation home—and put that picture where you will see it every day. I can attest to this being a strategy that really works. Choose your picture carefully.

We have a policy at our house: When I buy something that makes money, my wife is my partner, and if it loses money (like my boats and airplane), I need another partner. It's a great policy. Most toys such as boats and motor homes sit unattended for 95 percent of their lives. Having a partner or several not only cuts your cost, but it also gets the darn thing used more often, which increases the chances that it will start when you want to use it.

GOOD REASONS TO SELL

Houses grow old, neighborhoods change, and even landlords get tired of making money after a while. Here are some good reasons to sell a house:

1. *Neighborhood changing for the worse.* Neighborhoods have cycles. When owners sell and landlords buy in a neighborhood, property values often will drop. Sell when you see this happening, and you might be able to buy back in cheaper when the cycle reverses itself.
2. *Worn-out house.* It costs a lot of money and takes a lot of time to fix up a house that needs a new kitchen, baths, plumbing, roof, and so on. Most improvements you make only increase the value of a house by a fraction of what you spend. An investment in a new kitchen, one of the best things you can do, will increase the value of the house only by about 75 percent of what you spend. It is smarter to buy another house in good repair and sell your worn-out house to a buyer looking for a project. There are a lot of buyers in that category.
3. *Worn-out landlord.* Some landlords enjoy their work into their eighties. It is one job that you can keep for life if you want it. A smart landlord with 20 properties may work only an hour or two a month. You can delegate all the bad jobs. Just keep the ones that you like, such as going to the bank. Should you reach the point where you are not having any fun, consider selling to a family member whom you can teach the business or to another younger investor. See more details below.

BAD REASONS TO SELL

It can be a mistake to sell. Once you have bought a property that makes you money every month, don't sell it unless it is part of your plan.

1. *No leverage.* I have had financial advisors (who typically are trying to sell me insurance or stocks) tell me that owning free and clear properties is a terrible idea. Your rate of return is low. They are right to a point. What they do not consider is that if you own 10 houses, you can own 5 of them free and clear and 5 with loans and still have the benefit of leverage.

   Once you have enough property to produce all the cash flow you need, your focus should be to pay off your debt, not to borrow more. Remember, it is easier to borrow money than to pay it back.
2. *No depreciation.* If you own a house long enough, you will run out of depreciation. If the house is in a great neighborhood and making you money, keep it. Would you sell a stock that goes up every year and pays a big dividend? No, and it has no depreciation. If you want more depreciation, buy more property; don't sell off your winners.
3. *Someone wants to buy your house.* Someone always will want to buy your best properties. If you are going to sell one, sell your weakest property. Sell the one that attracts the worst tenants. When you begin to acquire properties, keep a list, with your favorite property at the top and your least favorite at the bottom. If you are married, share this with your spouse, and tell your spouse that if he or she ever needs to sell, sell the ones on the bottom of the list first.

HOW TO SELL

You can use an agent to sell your property or sell it yourself. If you have no selling skills, the agent may do a better job. If you will learn how to sell yourself, then you may be able to get as high a price as the agent or even higher and save the commission.

My favorite way to sell is described in Chapter 11. Selling on lease/options allows me to sell to a homeowner who is struggling to buy a house, often their first house, and yet sell at a retail price.

When you sell on a lease/option, you can have the buyers pay your closing costs, and you sell the house in its "as is" condition.

How Much Does Selling on Lease/Option Save You?

Here is a comparison of a lease/option sale and a sale through an agent:
Market value of house: $150,000–$160,000

	Through Realtor	With Lease /Option
Offering price	$159,950	$159,950
Sale price	$155,000	$159,950
Commission	$10,850	$0
Closing costs	$1,200	$0
Net proceeds	$142,950	$159,950
Date you receive the money	90–180 days	1 year+

The advantages of selling through a professional agent are that you are paid sooner and that you do not have to do the work of running an ad, talking to potential buyers, and then closing the deal. Not all houses listed for sale sell during the first listing period. You might have to wait the best part of a year to be paid, even selling through a good agent.

Learn how to sell your own houses using a lease/option, and you will make more money and be able to sell to a buyer who cannot qualify for a loan today or make a down payment as big as a commission.

Selling to a Family Member Using a Lease/Option

You may have a family member who is interested in investing but who is short of funds. You could sell that person a house that you want to sell using a lease/option. You could make them a good deal on both the rent and the price to give that person a better than average chance of making a profit. You could even help the person manage the property and provide a little advice along the way.

When selling to a family member, you could use a longer-term lease/option to give the person more time to make a profit. You might plan for your relative to refinance and pay you off when the property increases 50 percent in value. If in your town that would take about five years, you could use that term and then renegotiate if the person needed more time.

Should it not work out, then you would still own the house, and you probably would be out some rent that you did not collect. It is better to sell to a family member using a lease/option for a couple of reasons:

1. You don't have to report the sale on your tax return until the relative exercises the option to buy. If he doesn't buy, you still own it and have not had to report a sale.
2. You don't have to foreclose to recover title to the property. You would not want to foreclose on a family member.

Selling to Another Investor Using a Lease/Option

If you have no one in your family who wants to invest, there are many young investors getting started today who would eagerly buy from you on a lease/option. You could sell at a retail price without a commission. The investor then would manage the property and pay you when she resold it or refinanced it.

A good friend of mine who had accumulated many houses is systematically selling off his houses one at a time to young investors who attend an investment club with him. He is giving these young investors a chance to make a profit off their first house while selling at a good price without any advertising or expense. If they do not exercise their option and close, he still owns the house. He can choose to renegotiate the deal at a higher price and rent or sell to another.

15

Eight Steps to Quitting Your Day Job

Waking up in the morning excited about the prospects of the day rather than dreading the same old routine may be the best part of working for yourself. Working for others is limiting in many ways. You have to work certain hours on certain days. The type of work you do may not challenge you or let you reach your potential.

When you are the boss, you can set goals without limits. You can define your job to use your skills most productively. You can spend your time doing what you do best and delegate other tasks.

You can work 12 hours a day or 12 hours a week. The amount of money you make will be limited only by your knowledge (which you can acquire) and your dedication.

When you are excited about something and see unlimited potential in what you are doing, you will want to work, and your work will become fun. Work that you like to do and that is productive is extremely satisfying.

There are challenges in working for yourself. One is knowing when you are ready.

Working for others is not all bad news. There is security in a regular paycheck. Your job gives you an identity and may give you colleagues, things you may really miss when you are working alone. You also may have benefits, such as health insurance, sick leave, or a company car. Someone else is providing you with a place to work and the tools to work with. A job may be limiting and less exciting, but it is more predictable.

Working for yourself, and especially by yourself, takes commitment, organization, and focus. When you lose the structure of a job, you must recreate that structure, or you can spend a lot of time making coffee and looking out the windows.

The answers to these questions may influence your decision as to whether to go it on your own:

1. Do you have another source of income, such as a spouse's job, income from investments, or retirement pay from a previous career?
2. Have you bought and sold property for a profit?
3. Have you had success at managing property?
4. Have you saved enough cash to buy properties and to support yourself until your program supports you?

Unless you can answer yes to at least two of these questions, you may not be ready to jump out of your job and into an uncertain future. Having another source of income gives you a big advantage. You will get to eat regularly and keep up with the utility bills. But more important, it reduces the pressure to make a deal until the right one comes along.

Assuming that you are sufficiently motivated to start planning the transition, here is a plan you could use, based on the experiences of many investors who have gone before you.

EIGHT STEPS TO QUITTING YOUR DAY JOB

Step 1: Identify Your Skills and Weaknesses

You have developed skills that helped you with your job. Some of these same skills will help you as you enter full time into the world of real estate. Before moving on, list the skills that you have that you feel can help you in a new business.

It is possible to delegate some jobs. Most entrepreneurs do everything in the beginning. As business picks up, you begin to delegate the jobs that you are not good at and the ones that can be delegated easily. Early on, I discovered a deficiency in organizational abilities and hired a secretary/bookkeeper to keep files organized and the checkbooks balanced and reconciled.

Here is a short list of skills you need as a buyer, manager, and seller of property:

- Manager of people and money
- Negotiator
- An understanding of real estate law
- Bookkeeper/secretary
- Property appraiser
- Planner—the ability to put together an annual business plan and budget

Notice what I didn't list—handyman, yardman, plumber, tax expert, legal expert. Some jobs, such as the handyman, are skilled jobs, but they can be hired for a fraction of your earning potential. Other jobs, such as legal or tax experts, are too expensive to learn. Hire an attorney or accountant when you need one.

Jobs such as yard care and painting may be ones you can handle easily. Although you may justify spending a few hours repairing properties as you begin, it will soon become apparent that your time is better spent buying than repairing.

As a planner, it is your responsibility to put together an annual business plan. During the year, you need to evaluate and make adjustments in that plan to ensure success. In addition, you need to provide the tools and materials necessary to operate the business. One necessary ingredient is capital (money). As the boss, you have to provide it. You will establish a policy for dealing with your customers, employees, and suppliers. The attitude of your business depends on your management philosophy.

Negotiation is too expensive to delegate. It is the highest-paying job you can have. Negotiation also may be the hardest task to delegate well. Few people are good negotiators, and many individuals just don't like it.

Part of successful negotiation is negotiating from strength. When you are not under pressure to buy, sell, rent, or borrow, you are in a strong position to negotiate a good deal.

Negotiation skills can be learned. The libraries are full of books on negotiation. You have to practice to become a good negotiator. A strategy of making a lot of little deals rather than just one big one gives you the opportunity to practice and improve your negotiation skills. In negotiation for real estate, the details are important. If you are new to real estate and uninformed about contract law and your state's real estate laws, take a course or two at your community college and gain that knowledge. Knowledge is power.

Keeping good files and financial records, balancing and reconciling checkbooks monthly, and filing tax returns on schedule are all critical to a successful business. Many in business think that they are making money but end up broke because they thought a high gross income would produce a high net income. Other investors pay high fees to accountants to file tax returns from incomplete or disorganized records. Still other people pay attorneys to get them out of deals that were put together sloppily. If organization is not your skill, hire someone with that proficiency. You can find a part-time employee or contract with a bookkeeper/secretary to help you.

Knowing property values and the market for rents is important and, fortunately, easily learned. If you follow my advice and purchase houses in a narrow price range, then it will not take you long to learn prices and rents within that range. I suggest that you identify just a few neighborhoods that have houses in the price range in which you want to buy and then become an expert at values in those neighborhoods. Once in a while a really good deal comes along. You will be able to say yes in a hurry only if you are confident about the property values.

In the same neighborhoods, look at every house that becomes available for rent. Talk to the landlords. Ask how much deposit they want and who they will accept as tenants. Know your competition, and then have the best houses at the best prices, and you will stay full. Occasionally, you will find a landlord who wants to sell. You may be able to buy with owner financing on terms that will allow you to make a profit from the first day.

Do you have any weak areas among these first six? Identify what you need to do to obtain these critical skills. There is much more to learn, but this is where to start.

Step 2: Write Your Job Description

Would you take a job offer without knowing what your new job would be? Of course not. So how can you expect to switch to working for yourself without knowing what your new job will be like? I cannot write your job description, but let me share what an ad would look like if I wanted to replace myself:

> *Wanted CEO to Lead Company in Real Estate Acquisition, Financing, and Management*
>
> ***Responsibilities include: property acquisition, financing, and management of a portfolio of single-family homes. This includes hands-on negotiations with sellers, tenants, suppliers, and repairers. Also includes direct responsibility for all accounting and tax filings. Compensation to be commensurate with performance.***

Notice that the description does not include the number of hours per week required. Like most management jobs, there is no limit. Most investors who work for themselves put in many more hours than when they were employed by others. You should give this some thought, especially if you are raising a family.

Working for Yourself Does Not Have to Mean Giving Up Life as You Know It

I set a policy early in my career to never conduct business after hours or on weekends. No buying, no selling, no tenant calls. It would be too easy to choose work over family. Although an occasional emergency pops up, it is the exception, not the rule. You can make a good living working 40 to 60 hours a week. If you are single or your kids are grown and you are working as a team, then work as long as you are having fun. But don't give up your family life because you now work for yourself.

The flip side of this is that you do have to work productively 40 to 60 hours a week to operate a growing business that will produce significant profits. You should develop both a daily work plan and a long-term plan. This plan would set out what you want to accomplish and how you intend to accomplish it.

A work plan for a day when you are determined to buy a house might be to get up early and drive to a neighborhood in which you have an interest. Take three hours to walk through the neighborhood, talking to neighbors, knocking on doors of houses that need attention, and noting vacant houses and brokers who are working the area. After lunch, you might spend the time on your computer or at the courthouse looking up the ownership of the properties you found and, if you have time, trying to contact the owners. This day's work should produce several real leads.

You also should contact the brokers active in the area to see if they have any empty houses listed by sellers who want to see all offers. Also try to identify a broker who handles foreclosures in the area. Often one broker will specialize in foreclosures. He needs several buyers, and you could be one.

Step 3: Inventory Your Assets

Prepare a financial statement. This will give you a snapshot of where you are today. With a little projection, you can figure out where you need to go. Let's look at your financial statement and see what assets you have that will help as you start your own business.

- *Cash on hand.* Although cash is necessary to pay the bills and put food on the table, large amounts of cash are not necessary to purchase real estate. Sellers and other lenders are willing to loan you a large percentage of the purchase price of properties you want to buy. You should have some accumulated cash, and more important, you should have a habit of saving cash. If you are constantly short of cash, you are spending more than you make. If you can't adjust your income, then you should adjust your spending to allow for some savings every month.
- *Property owned.* Property you now own, such as the home you live in, may give you the ability to raise cash to buy other properties.

You may own other assets, such as a vehicle or life insurance, that are easy to borrow against. It is often easier to refinance than borrow against a new property. However, refinancing is not a profit-making strategy, and this is a bad habit to develop. Having equity that you can borrow against in a pinch gives you a safety blanket.

- *Established credit.* Your financial statement also will show whom you now owe. If you have established credit with a bank or a private lender, you may be able to borrow more from that source. The ability to borrow replaces your need to have a lot of cash on hand. Good credit allows you to borrow at cheaper interest rates. Protect your good credit by always repaying on time.
- *Investors.* Knowing other people who have money that they want to invest safely is an asset that won't show on your financial statement. Once you learn to structure safe, high-profit deals, then you can use investor money instead of your own money for down payments and borrowed money.

Step 4: Form a Plan to Replace Your Income

Do you have current investments that can replace some of the income from your job? You can replace your income with two sources: investment income and business income. The investment income from rents, sales of investment property, and interest eventually can replace all of your earned income. At that point, you will be able to live entirely on your investment income. In the short term, you may need to buy and sell properties to produce some business income on which to live.

Most investors accumulate a number of investment properties before they decide to quit their jobs. When you own property, you have rental income plus the ability to sell or refinance if you need cash.

Having the experience of buying and managing houses increases your confidence that you can do more. You may even have the thought of one of my friends, "Why should I stay on this job when I could be making so much more if I spent the same 40 hours a week buying houses?"

Here is a combination business/investment plan to replace a salary of $60,000:

1. Buy and sell six houses at an average profit of $10,000.
2. Buy and hold two additional houses with net monthly cash flows of $100 each.

As your investment properties produce more income, you can buy and sell fewer houses and buy and hold more for long-term profits. As your skill level increases, you will find that you can make significantly more than $10,000 profit on your average house. Work toward lower volume and higher profits.

Step 5: Accumulate a Cash Reserve

Many new businesses fail because they are undercapitalized. This means that the owners did not start with enough cash to last long enough to be successful. There is a learning curve in every business. Hopefully, the longer you are in business, the wiser you will become. The key is to last long enough to get smart.

The amount of money you need to start with depends on two factors. The first is your ability to start generating income. If you know how to buy and sell, then you can begin generating income almost immediately.

Selling a Contract to Another Investor

One way to make a few thousand dollars in only a few days is to contract to buy a house at a below-market price and then assign that contract to another investor for a profit. The amount of profit you can command will depend on how good of a deal you made and how good a negotiator you are when you sell.

Many investors are looking for property. If you develop the skills and do the work to find bargains and to negotiate both a good price and good terms, you can sell your position in these contracts for a profit.

If you are just beginning, you may not have the skill to buy far enough below the market to be able to sell at a quick profit to another investor. You can develop this skill by following my advice on looking for property and then by making offers to motivated sellers. You will be surprised at how quickly you can begin buying property at bargain prices.

This strategy of buying and selling for a small profit is just a transitional strategy to provide short-term cash flow while you accumulate other, more profitable properties. You will learn to buy properties that you can resell after holding them for several years for much larger profits.

The second factor is your lifestyle and the amount you need to live. If you are single and can live cheaply, you can get by on a few dollars a month. It's amazing how cheap you can live if it becomes a game.

Many single investors start off by buying or renting a house and then renting out the rooms for enough to make the payments so that they get to live there free. They learn the sources of free coffee, cheap meals, and free entertainment. They drive cheap-to-operate and -insure vehicles. They wear casual clothes. They do this in order to invest every dime they can in property.

If you are raising a family and have obligations such as mortgage payments, you need a steadier and larger supply of cash on hand for day-to-day expenses and emergencies. Break your monthly expenses into two categories—"nice to have" and "must have." All adults in the family must be willing to live without the first group for a while for this to work.

Starting with six months' pay in the bank is standard wisdom, but I would adjust it by the preceding factors. I would increase it if I had a family depending on me. I might decrease it if I knew that I had the ability to borrow money.

Just before quitting his job, one friend of mine sold two houses that he had been holding as investments. He put the money in the bank for security. Interestingly, he never touched it, but it was there if he needed it. It gave him the confidence to make the move.

Other investors have taken money from their retirement plans. If you have the option to take retirement plan money, don't take it unless you need it. Even when it's in the plan, it can be your security blanket.

Step 6: Transition (Don't Leap)

All good things have a gestation period. Becoming your own boss is a process, not an event. Getting to the point where you can confidently and comfortably leave your job, knowing that the worst-case scenario is survivable, is a process. It requires going through some of the steps just discussed.

Most investors I talk to have a two-year plan (or longer) to quit their job. During that period, they plan to accumulate both the skills and the assets (such as a cash reserve and credit) that they need. If your plan includes buying and selling property to generate cash flow, then you should buy and sell several houses profitably before you quit. You need to prove—mostly to yourself—that you can do it.

Some plans even include relocating. A good friend who took my class several years ago was a practicing dentist. After buying a number of properties, he began complaining about the hassles of practicing dentistry, so over dinner one night I suggested that he quit.

He had never thought about making a change that radical in his life. After a lot of thought, he not only quit, but he also decided to move to another state where real estate had more potential. He exchanged his properties tax-free for newer properties in a better area.

You will never be completely ready or have all the answers. At some point you will have to take a leap of faith. When you do, you will have some days when you think you were crazy to quit and others when you can't believe it took you so long.

Step 7: Replace Your Old Benefits with New Ones

When you leave a job, you may be leaving behind benefits that were tax-free to you. Health insurance paid by your employer, a company car, and a company computer, are typical benefits offered to employees.

You typically can continue your medical coverage, but at your own expense. Although your employer was paying for your health insurance with before-tax dollars, you will now be paying taxes and then paying the premiums.

You can have the same benefits that you had with your old job if you incorporate and take advantage of the same tax breaks that benefit other corporations like General Motors. Your corporation should be in business, not investing. The business may be one of buying and selling properties, or it could be one of managing your properties.

Either way, the company will generate gross profits that can be used to pay employee benefits such as you had on your old job. If you are the only employee, your benefits may even be more liberal than before. Check with your accountant to establish bounds of reasonableness.

By having your business pay for expenses such as telephone, computers, automobile expenses, health insurance, business travel and entertainment, and others, you may need much less personal income to pay expenses.

Step 8: Find a Mentor or Support Group

One big challenge you will face, especially if you have been working with others, is working alone. You have not only lost the corporate identity you had with the company, but now you also have to deal with being isolated. A solution is to identify a mentor, someone who has done what you aspire to do. You need to find a person you can sit down with on a regular basis and talk about the challenges you are facing.

In addition, find a larger support group, such as a monthly investment club. Or you could put together a small group of like-minded investors who might meet once a week for a meal. Being able to bounce your ideas off others can be invaluable.

CONTINUE YOUR EDUCATION

Improve your skills to improve your profits and so that you will continue to be enthusiastic. Set an annual budget for attending conventions, taking seminars, buying books, and simply traveling to study other markets. Get out of your town several times a year, and study the markets in other towns. You will return home excited, and reenergized.

After more than 30 years as a student of real estate investing, I continue to learn new ways to make money every year. This new information and new way of looking at investments keeps me excited about investing. Keep learning and you will make more money than your competition and stay excited about what you are doing.

16

HOW TO OWN THE HOUSE OF YOUR DREAMS FREE AND CLEAR

You may have heard that the house you live in can be your best investment. This can be true—if it is your only investment. Other investments can outperform your home, and the house you live in has some serious flaws as an investment.

First, think about your house from a cash-flow standpoint. The only kind of cash flow your house will produce is negative cash flow—money going out for taxes, for insurance, for repairs, for remodeling, and for loan payments. The house you live in is a constant and major drain on your checkbook.

Even if you own your house free and clear of all debt (which I recommend), it will cost you plenty to own it. You can get cash flow from your home by renting out rooms, which is really converting your home to an investment property, but most of us do not want roommates.

A second way to get cash flow from your house is to borrow against it. But this will create even bigger monthly payments to be paid unless you are old enough to make sense of a reverse mortgage.

A *reverse mortgage* is a loan that pays you, rather than requiring that you make payments. A reverse mortgage typically is used by homeowners with a relatively few years left in their home. The payments you receive are based on your remaining life expectancy and would be low if you had many years to live. This is an excellent way to use the equity in your personal residence to increase your cash flow.

My friend Robert Bruss has championed reverse mortgages. If you want to learn more about them, his Web site is Robertbruss.com. He writes the popular "Real Estate Mailbag" and Real Estate Law columns syndicated nationally, and an excellent newsletter.

THE FIRST BIG MISTAKE, BUYING TOO MUCH HOUSE

Do you know someone who has spent all his or her money buying a big house and now can't even afford furniture? Several of my friends have taken this path.

Many home buyers make the mistake of buying the most expensive house they can afford for their first home. Agents, of course, have a financial incentive to sell a more expensive house, and lenders also have financial incentives to make the largest loans possible. Home buyers get a lot of encouragement to stretch and buy the most house they can afford.

Even the tax code encourages taxpayers to take on a large mortgage so that they can deduct the interest and protect some of their income from taxes. What most people do not understand is that interest is not a "tax shelter"; it is a deductible expense, like property taxes. You want to minimize your expenses, deductible or not, because you have to write a check for them before you can deduct them.

Unfortunately, all this advice often lands the new buyers in a house that will consume their every extra nickel for years. This leaves them with nothing to invest. It also leaves them vulnerable to downturns in the economy. When unemployment increases, the number of foreclosures increases. The newest home buyers are the most likely to lose their homes and their good credit in foreclosure.

HOW TO OWN THE HOUSE OF YOUR DREAMS FREE AND CLEAR

Early in my career I made a decision to rent a house to live in and to use my cash and the monthly cash flow I saved by not buying a personal residence to buy investment properties. I was able to live in a home that I rented in one of the best neighborhoods in my town for a small fraction of what it would have cost me to own it. I was able to live beyond my means and take the cash that I did not use to buy a home and invest it.

Over nine years, I accumulated a significant number of investment properties. The properties—purchased and managed carefully as outlined in this book—produced cash flow. The depreciation allowance on investment property produced a real tax shelter that I could use to avoid paying taxes on my other income. And the houses resulted in a growing net worth. Nine years after I began investing, I bought the house of my dreams and was able to pay cash for it. I still live there 24 years later.

Compare these two plans: plan A, buying a nice house to live in today, and plan B, renting a house to live in today and buying at least one investment property a year. I have chosen house values for this example that are round numbers. If the numbers are way off for your area, try doubling them if you are in a higher-priced market or using half if your houses are less expensive. Don't get hung up on the numbers—get the concept.

Plan A: Buy the House of Your Dreams Today

House value:	$250,000
Purchase price:	$250,000 (Most buyers pay retail or near retail when they buy a house they really like.)
Down payment:	$12,500
Closing costs:	$6,000
Total cash to move in:	$18,500
Monthly payments (30-year fixed loan at 6.5%):	$1,498.52
Estimated taxes and insurance ($3,600 annual):	$300

Estimated maintenance and repairs and replacements (carpeting, paint,etc.; $2,400 annual):	$200
Total estimated monthly cost:	–$1,998.52
Hold this house until it doubles in value:	10 years ("guestimate")
Value in 10 years:	$500,000
Loan balance in 10 years (without refinancing):	$209,271
Equity in 10 years (without refinancing):	$290,728
Cash flow during the 10 years:	–$1,998.52 per month, plus increases in taxes and insurance, and any major remodeling

Now $290,000 in equity is a substantial amount. It is far more than most people ever accumulate, but it is far less than you can accumulate if you have a better plan. Study plan B.

Plan B: Buy One Investment House a Year for 10 Years, and Then Buy the House of Your Dreams for Cash

Year One:	Buy one house
House value:	$125,000
Purchase price:	$110,000 (Don't buy unless you can buy at at least 10% below the market)
Down payment:	$10,000 (Not more than 10% down)
Closing costs:	$3,000
Total cash to close:	$13,000
Loan balance:	$ 90,000
Monthly payments (30-year fixed loan at 7.5%):	$629.29

Estimated taxes and insurance ($1,800 annually):	$150
Estimated maintenance and repairs and replacements (carpeting, paint, etc.; $1,200 annual):	$100
Total estimated monthly cost:	$879.29
Estimated monthly rent (year one):	$950
Projected monthly cash flow the first 12 months:	+$70.71
Hold this house until it doubles in value:	10 years ("guesstimate")
Value in 10 years:	$250,000
Loan balance in 10 years (without refinancing):	$78,115
Equity in 10 years (without refinancing):	$171,884
Year two:	Buy another house
House value:	$134,000 (Same house/same neighborhood—includes 7.2% appreciation)
Purchase price:	$120,000 (Don't buy unless you can buy at at least 10% below the market)
Down payment:	$12,000 (Not more than 10% down)
Closing costs:	$3,000
Total cash to close:	$15,000
Loan balance:	$105,000
Monthly payments (30-year fixed loan at 7.5%):	$734.17

Estimated taxes and insurance ($1,920 annually):	$160
Estimated maintenance and repairs and replacements (carpeting, paint, etc.; $1,296 annual):	$108
Total estimated monthly cost:	$1,002.17
Estimated monthly rent:	$1,025 (year one)
Projected monthly cash flow the first 12 months:	+$22.83
Hold this house until it doubles in value:	10 years ("guestimate")
Value in 10 years:	$268,000
Loan balance in 10 years (without refinancing):	$91,135
Equity in 10 years (without refinancing):	$176,865

Year three:	Buy third house
House value:	$144,000
Purchase price:	$129,000 (Don't buy unless you can buy at at least 10% below the market)
Down payment:	$10,000 (Not more than 10% down)
Closing costs:	$4,000
Total cash to close:	$14,000
Loan balance:	$115,000
Monthly payments (30-year fixed loan at 7.5%):	$804.10
Estimated taxes and insurance ($1,920 annually):	$160
Estimated maintenance and repairs and replacements (carpeting, paint, etc.; $1,296 annual):	$108

Total estimated monthly cost:	$1,072.10
Estimated monthly rent:	$1,100 (year one)
Projected monthly cash flow the first 12 months:	+$37.90
Hold this house until it doubles in value:	10 years
Value in 10 years:	$288,000
Loan balance in 10 years (without refinancing):	$99,814
Equity in 10 years (without refinancing):	$188,186

Table 16.1 shows all 10 houses that you would purchase and the values, loan balances, and equities after the first 10 years. The first house has doubled in value. The second house has increased in value only 9 years, so it has not yet doubled. Even though the last house you purchased in year 10 has not appreciated at all, you did purchase it at 10 percent below the market and made a down payment. Your equity is a combination of the discount you earned when you bought the house and the amount of your down payment. Actually, you will become a better buyer each year and make purchases at larger discounts as you improve your buying skills. You also may learn to buy with lower down payments, stretching your cash further.

All these numbers have been rounded to make it easier to understand. It is impossible to make an accurate 10-year projection, but it is possible to compare plan A and plan B using the same assumption, namely, that property will double in value in 10 years. Don't worry about the inaccuracy of the projection. Compare the performance of the two portfolios.

What would your net worth be with each plan? Would you have enough equity with plan "B" to buy the house of your dreams for all cash?

Compare the cash flows. Recognize that rents also will increase with property values over a 10-year period.

If you need money during the first 10 years, would it be easier to sell a rental house to get the money or to sell the house that you live in?

Table 16.1 The Effect of Buying One House a Year

Year Purchased	Market Value When Purchased	Purchase Price	Value 10 Years After First House Purchased	Loan Balance in 10 Years	Your Equity in 10 Years
1	$125,000	$110,000	$250,000	$78,115	$171,885
2	$134,000	$120,000	$250,000	$93,031	$156,969
3	$144,000	$129,000	$250,000	$103,820	$146,180
4	$154,000	$139,000	$250,000	$117,548	$132,452
5	$165,000	$148,000	$250,000	$126,730	$123,270
6	$177,000	$160,000	$250,000	$139,916	$110,084
7	$189,000	$170,000	$250,000	$151,387	$98,613
8	$203,000	$183,000	$250,000	$165,839	$84,161
9	$218,000	$196,000	$250,000	$180,447	$69,553
10	$234,000	$211,000	$250,000	$196,169	$53,831
11	$250,000	$225,000	$250,000	$210,000	$40,000
Totals:			$2,750,000	$1,563,002	$1,186,998

Funding the Down Payments

Where will you get the down payment to buy the 10 houses?

- Part can come from the money you do not use to buy a house to live in.
- Another part can come from the cash flow that the rental houses will generate.
- A third part can come from the real tax shelter that the rental houses will generate and that you can use to reduce your tax liability.
- Another part can come from money you won't spend decorating, buying furniture, and remodeling the house you live in while you are renting.

RENTING THE HOUSE OF YOUR DREAMS FOR A SONG

It may seem funny, but you often can rent a nicer house for less than you would pay for a cheaper house. I have done it and have helped students negotiate terrific deals to rent larger homes in the nicest neighborhoods in town.

Less expensive houses are in great demand, and you will have competition to rent them. More expensive houses are in less demand; you will have less competition for such a house and will be able to negotiate a better deal.

If you owned a nice home in good condition but were not going to live in it yourself for several years, who would you want to rent it to? Would you rent it to a group of college students who would pay a little extra monthly rent to have a really nice place to hold parties?

Or would you rather rent it to a mature, responsible tenant who would take great care of your home, even though he would not pay nearly as much rent? Would you net more after expenses renting to the college kids or to a responsible tenant for half as much a month? Which tenant would allow you to sleep better?

I found the last house we rented by driving through the best neighborhood in my town. I wanted to live there, and I was looking for an empty house that I could rent. It took several weeks of looking, but I found the house: It was empty, owned by the heir of an estate, and it was for rent.

A Realtor had a sign in the yard and was asking $1,100 a month (this was in the 1970s). The house was on a great lot, but it needed some work. I offered to pay $650 a month if the owner would make improvements such as new carpeting and new paint and remodel the kitchen. The Realtor was so embarrassed by my offer that she would not present it. She had told the owner that she could get $1,100 a month. Instead, she gave me the out-of-town owner's name and number and asked me to call him directly.

I was happy to call the owner and have some conversations so that we could get to know each other. We struck a deal where I would take the house in "as is" condition and make the improvements that I wanted, and he would rent the house to me for four years at $300 per month, including lawn care.

I'm not sure, but I suspect that the Realtor fell off her chair when she learned of the deal I made. While the Realtor did not understand the reason that an owner would rent at a bargain price, it made perfect sense to me as a landlord.

The owner wanted a tenant that would take care of the house and not make a lot of demands. I was his dream tenant. Having the right tenant was far more important than getting more money. The Realtor had not produced any tenant at the $1,100 price, so I suspect the owner knew that the price was too high to start with.

If you want to rent a house to live in, look in the better neighborhoods in your town. Look for a house that has been empty for a while, and if it would work for you, make an offer to lease it for several years at a below-market price. A multiple-year lease has many advantages to both the owner and you. You won't have to move, and your rent won't increase. The owner does not have to worry about vacancies or advertising and maintaining an empty house for several years.

Offer to take the house in "as is" condition and to be responsible for minor maintenance of the house. You can define minor maintenance in dollar terms, for instance, anything that costs less than $75 to repair. If the house is now offered at a high rental price, don't let that deter you from making an offer that makes sense to you. You bring more to the table than just money. You bring peace of mind, and as they say in the ad, "That's priceless."

You can save hundreds and even thousands of dollars a month by renting rather than owning this house. Then use the saved money to invest in other property that will make you more money. Another advantage is that you don't have to pay the ever-increasing costs of taxes and insurance or worry about major repair bills.

I rented two different houses, both at well below-market rents, one for five years and one for four years, before I bought my own home. The money I saved by renting and by not spending a lot of money on the house I lived in allowed me to buy enough properties that when I did buy "my home," I was able to pay cash for it and make a good deal.

actually make a small profit. If he wants to own an investment with a positive cash flow, he can refinance the existing loan at a lower rate or for a longer term or renegotiate the loan, paying enough down so that the rent will cover the cost today.

The test of a good deal is whether it is a good deal for both parties involved. Would you agree that both Jack and Charlie have a good deal?

17

TAKE CHARGE OF YOUR RETIREMENT INCOME

Do you know someone who is working at a job that they don't like just to get retirement benefits? There is a lot of risk in this strategy because some companies may underfund their retirement plans and be unable to fulfill their obligations to their long-time employees.

Other companies file for bankruptcy and their employees receive far less in retirement benefits than they counted on. In today's world, it is risky to depend on either a company or the government for your retirement income.

Although the Social Security System is likely to be around for many years to come, it is also likely that the age to receive benefits will increase, and the amount of the benefits you may receive will be less than you need to live comfortably.

Real estate, specifically well-located houses, can provide a growing source of retirement income. It is income that will protect you from the ravages of inflation.

How long do you have to work for a company or the government to qualify for retirement benefits? Is it possible to work for 20 years and then still have less than you need for retirement? In less than 20 years you can generate enough income from investing in a few houses that will exceed the income from nearly any retirement plan.

A 10-YEAR RETIREMENT PLAN THAT YOU CAN COUNT ON

Countless investors are now enjoying the benefits of this plan in far less time than it would take to earn a pension. Since this is their plan and they are in charge and in control of their retirement funds, they sleep better than those who have to rely on others to manage their retirement money.

Because houses in good areas continue to appreciate, rather than sell a good-performing house to capture your profits, it makes more sense to take your profits out in a loan.

Two of the big advantages of investing in houses are (1) money that you borrow against a house is tax-free, and (2) houses make good collateral for loans. In fact, a good house in a good neighborhood is your banker's favorite collateral for a loan simply because it continues to appreciate in value. If you were a banker, would you rather lend against a car or boat that drops in value 20 percent its first week or a house that continues to appreciate?

Because houses appreciate over time and make great collateral, you do not have to sell good houses to get your profit. You can borrow it, but you must have a well-thought-out plan, or you can borrow yourself into bankruptcy.

Following is a plan I have taught to students for nearly 30 years. It worked for me and for many who decided to take charge of their own retirement rather than trust the government or an employer.

Suppose that you bought a house like the one I used in the 10/10/10 example in Chapter 4 and you held it until it doubled in value. To be on the conservative side, I will assume that your loan has been paid down only $2,250 during the time the house doubled in value.

Market value when you bought:	$150,000
Your purchase price:	$135,000
Your down payment:	$13,500
Your loan:	$122,500

Now, after a period of time, the house has doubled in value as the loan has been paid down. In a good credit market, an investor with good credit typically can borrow 80 percent of the appraised value.

The money you receive from borrowing against a house is tax-free. If you need $80,000 a year to live on, you would have to earn much more than $80,000 if it was taxable. You can borrow just the $80,000 because you pay no taxes on borrowed money.

Borrow only the amount that the tenants can afford to repay. This will vary with the interest rates and terms available to you. You want the rents to repay this loan because you want to continue to hold this house until it doubles again.

When the house has doubled in value:

Today's market value:	$300,000
Old loan balance:	$120,000
New loan available:	$240,000
Less old loan payoff:	$120,000
Less closing cost on new loan:	$6,000
Net available from refinancing:	$114,000

How long would you have to work to qualify for an *after-tax* retirement benefit of $114,000 a year? The truth is that only a handful of people ever qualify for this kind of retirement income.

For this plan to work, you need more than one house. If houses typically double in value every 10 years in your town, you need 10 houses. Buying and managing 10 houses may sound like a lot, but its not a full-time job. You can easily buy and manage 10 good houses that attract good tenants while still working full time. The secret is buying the right houses and learning how to finance them so that you can afford to buy them and manage them well. Buy one house at a time, so you can learn slowly how to negotiate and manage property. You can do it. Thousands have done so successfully and are doing it every day.

> My best friend's secretary recently retired at the age of 52. She and her husband began following my plan of buying one house a year several years ago and now own nine houses, almost all free and clear. The nine houses produce more net income than both of them have ever earned in a year together. If they want more cash today for retirement, they can refinance a house when the interest rates are favorable. It's a simple plan, and it works.

OWNING THE HOUSES THAT WILL MAKE YOU THE MOST MONEY LONG TERM

You can increase your capital gains income dramatically by buying more expensive properties. You can buy these properties at great dollar discounts because there is less competition to buy them. Most investors buy less expensive properties, so it is harder to get a bargain on a less expensive house.

If you are able to buy an $80,000 house for $60,000, the $20,000 profit is a great deal in that price range. If you are buying a $240,000 house, a great deal may be a price of $180,000, a $60,000 profit; three times as much as the smaller house. You can control much more real estate and make greater profits when you buy more expensive houses.

Compare these two real houses in my town today:

Value today:	$80,000	$240,000
Rents today:	$800–$900	$1,200–$1,600
Market value 30 years ago:	$20,000	$30,000
Rents 30 years ago:	$175–$225	$250–$275

I owned both these houses. I sold the less expensive house and still own the more expensive one, but I have tracked them both.

Notice that while the less expensive house has doubled in value twice ($20,000 to $40,000 and then $40,000 to $80,000), the more expensive house has doubled three times ($30,000 to $60,000, $60,000 to $120,000, and $120,000 to $240,000) during the same period of time. The more expensive house has attracted longer-term tenants and is actually easier to manage than the less expensive house. It's less work, and it produces far more profit.

BALANCING YOUR CASH FLOW NEEDS AND PROFITS FROM APPRECIATION

If you are starting out with little money, and cash flow today is important to you, buy a less expensive house. It will produce more of its profit in short-term cash flow. You can then use this cash flow to buy better properties.

If you have cash flow from another source and you are paying income taxes now, you can start buying better-located, more-expensive houses. With these houses, more of your profits will come in the form of long-term capital gain, taxed at a lower rate. A bonus is that if you leverage the house, it can produce a tax shelter today to offset your other income.

An advantage of investing in several houses rather than one big building is that you can buy some houses for cash flow and other property for maximum capital gains and tax shelter today. If you start buying less-expensive houses, you can sell them and reinvest without paying taxes in better-located houses as your cash flow increases. This will allow you to control more profits with fewer houses, fewer tenants, and less work.

18

GETTING YOUR HOUSES FREE AND CLEAR

SETTING YOUR GOAL FOR FREE AND CLEAR HOUSES

The first step is to set a goal for the number of free and clear houses that you want to own. Work backwards into this goal by first setting an income goal and then asking how many free and clear houses you will need to produce that target income.

For example, suppose that the house you would like to buy in your town produces rent in the $1,000 to $1,200 per month range and has operating expenses equal to about 30 percent of the gross rent. How many houses would you need?

One house (rental income $1,000 per month):	$12,000 per year
Operating expenses:	$3,600 per year
Net income:	$8,400 per year

Building Wealth One House at a Time

Annual Income Needed	Number of Free and Clear Houses Needed
$50,000	6
$100,000	12
$150,000	18
$200,000	24

Use real numbers in your town, and then make a projection using today's values and income of how many houses you will need. As rents increase with inflation, this income will provide you with the same lifestyle, even as prices increase dramatically over time.

These income projections assume that you never sell a house. You can increase your income even more by systematically selling some houses.

In researching, I found that most people who accumulate significant assets during their lifetimes become more conservative as they age and end up with most of these assets in their estates.

Unless you have a reason to leave a large estate, you can sell some of your assets and spend or give away the money while you are alive. One of my favorite preachers likes to say, "Do your giving while you're living, so you're know'n where it's going." People who discover the joy of giving really get a kick out of making gifts that help others change their lives. Give while you are alive to see how your gift makes a difference.

If you supplement your rental income with income from sales of properties, you can meet your financial goals quicker and do it with fewer properties than if you depend only on the rental income.

Suppose that at age 60 you own 20 houses; 10 that are free and clear and 10 with amortizing loans. The loans on the 10 financed houses all will be paid off within the next 20 years.

Your plan is to produce the greatest possible income during the next 20 years so that you can enjoy those years to their fullest, and then at age 80, you want to own 10 free and clear properties to support you comfortably for the rest of your life.

During the next 20 years, you plan to sell 10 houses to increase your income, keeping the remaining 10 houses for your more passive retirement years. Today each house is worth about $150,000. Your plan is to sell one every two years on average to increase your income by about $75,000 (in today's money) per year. You can adjust this strategy to get the best prices by selling only in strong real estate markets.

THREE PLANS FOR GETTING YOUR HOUSES FREE AND CLEAR

Plan 1: Use the Increased Cash Flow from Increasing Rents to Pay Off the Debt

How many years will it take you to pay off a 30-year loan? Thirty years if you make the same payment each month for 30 years. If you increase the amount of the payment you make as you raise your rents; you can pay off your loans much sooner.

As you acquire property with fixed payments, amortizing loans, your cash flow will increase each year as you increase your rents. You can use the increasing cash flow from one house to pay off the debt on that house.

If your rents increase at an average of 5 percent a year and you use that increase to make additional principal payments on your loan, you can pay off a 30-year loan in just over 14 years. Table 18.1 shows what your payment schedule would look like if you applied your increasing rent to your loan each year. The original loan is a 30-year $150,000 loan with 7 percent interest and payments of $997.75.

Although this is a simple plan and it works, it is not the quickest way to pay off the debt on your houses. It is a better plan to use the cash flow that the house produces to continue to buy other houses until you have the number of houses that, if paid for, will produce the cash flow that you need.

When you pay off a loan with an interest rate of 7 percent, you are investing your money at that 7 percent rate. If you buy another house with a small down payment, the return you will make on your investment during the first few years will be 40, 60, or even 100 percent. You can then use those profits to pay off your loans, and you can pay them off faster.

If you make prepayments of principal on any loan, keep careful records of your extra payments. It would be wiser and easier to keep track of if you just made one larger prepayment of principal each year rather than making increased monthly payments. For example, in year two,

Table 18.1 Paying off your 30-year loans in less than 15 years

Year	Rent Collected/Payment Made	Loan Balance at Year End
1	$997.75	$148,607
2	$1,050	$146,394
3	$1,155	$142,775
4	$1,215	$138,103
5	$1,276	$132,338
6	$1,338	$125,390
7	$1,405	$117,114
8	$1,475	$107,376
9	$1,550	$96,010
10	$1,628	$82,858
11	$1,709	$67,776
12	$1,794	$50,512
13	$1,884	$30,911
14	$1,978	$8,478
15	$2,077	$0

rather than making 12 payments of $1,050, you could make one prepayment of $600 at the end of the year. You would pay a few dollars more interest during the year, but the 14-year payoff plan would still work.

Bank bookkeepers do make mistakes, and when you make many unusual payments, they may not record them accurately and give you the proper credit. Keep your own records, keep proof of your payments, and make your own amortization schedule using programs that are widely available.

Plan 2: Buy More Houses Than You Really Want and Sell Off Some to Pay Off the Rest

Knowing that you can make more than a 7 percent return when you buy a house as an investment, a better plan is to use the profits that your houses will generate to buy additional houses. This will take more work; buying and managing more houses, but the results can be spectacular.

If using the same cash flow as in the preceding example we took the excess cash and bought more houses, here is an example of how the plan would work: Year 1, buy the first house. Years 2 through 10, buy another house each year using the cash flow from the earlier houses to provide down payments and to fund any cash-flow shortages in the new houses that you buy.

Remember the 10/10/10 rule? Here is an example of how the equity would grow in the first house that you bought if you did a little better than 10/10/10. You will do better as you practice making offers and learn your market.

Market value when you bought:	$180,000
Your purchase price:	$160,000
Your down payment:	$10,000
Your loan:	$150,000

Using a conservative rate of growth of 5 percent, let's look at the value and the debt after just 10 years:

Projected market value (at 5% growth):	$320,000
Loan balance in 10 years:	$125,920
Equity in property:	$194,080

It's hard to project what income tax rates will be in 10 years, but even after taxes, you should be able to sell one house, gross $194,000, pay taxes, and pay off another house that will have a loan balance of about the same $125,920.

Rather than waiting 14 years to pay off a loan using the increased rents, this plan allows you to get a house free and clear in 10 years at a conservative 5 percent rate of growth.

Plan 3: Refinance Some Property to Pay Off Others

If you follow plan 2 and continue to buy houses at below-market prices and with good financing, you will one day own a number of houses. Each will have a different loan balance and a different payment schedule. Some of these loans will have better interest rates and terms than others.

Take the time to carefully study the payments and amounts on all your loans and compare them. Which loans have the largest payments compared with the amount that you owe?

Suppose that you owned three houses with the following loans:

House	Market Value	Loan Amount	Loan Payment
1	200,000	100,000	700
2	200,000	100,000	900
3	200,000	100,000	1,200

Without knowing the interest rate on the loans, which would you want to pay off first? Obviously, the one with the highest payments. You can invest the same $100,000 and increase your monthly cash flow by more by paying off the loan with the largest payment. The interest rate is not as important as the ratio between the amount that you owe and the amount of the monthly payment.

As loans get older, their balances pay down, but the monthly payments remain the same. House 3 may have started with a $150,000 loan that has been paid down to $100,000.

If you are going to refinance one or more properties to pay off another, either refinance or pay off the loans with the highest payments to increase your cash flow.

Looking again at the house in the preceding example:

Projected market value in 10 years (at 5% growth):	$320,000
Loan balance in 10 years:	$125,920
Equity in property:	$194,080

Banks generally will lend investors 80 percent of the market value when you refinance a property. If you refinanced this house with a new 80 percent loan, you would be able to borrow $256,000.

If you owned another house with about the same loan balance of $126,000, you could pay off the loans on those two houses by refinancing just one house.

Now you would own one house free and clear and one with an 80 percent loan. If you can refinance when rates are low, you should be able to cover your payment with the rent that one house produces.

Owning a house free and clear and one with an 80 percent loan is a much safer position than having a $125,000 loan against both houses. When you have a large loan balance, the lender will not want to foreclose and will work with you in the event you have financial difficulties. When you have a small loan balance, the lender will gladly foreclose, confident that they will be repaid.

Another advantage is that, replacing two old loans with a new 30-year loan will reduce your payment. If you can borrow at a lower interest rate, it will drop even more.

A third advantage is, because you have not sold a house, you will pay no taxes. Because you have not sold, you still have both houses earning money for you.

You can use all three strategies, depending on the market, your desire to own a certain number of properties, and your need for cash flow. One thing is certain: You will change your plan if you start today and invest for the next 10 years. You will continue to learn more and will find ways to make even higher returns with your cash.

Know that what I have covered in this book is just the beginning of what you can learn about investing. There is much more to learn and more profitable opportunities available at another level of investing. The first step to get to that level is to begin acquiring wealth today, one house at a time.

19

BUYING AND OWNING OUT-OF-TOWN PROPERTY

I have owned property in 10 states with varying degrees of success. If you now own or are considering buying property out of your area, here are some tips on both buying and managing out-of-town property.

GOOD REASONS TO BUY OUT-OF-TOWN PROPERTY

There are several reasons that you may want to consider investing in another location. The best reason is to make more money than you can with property in your town. Jimmy Napier lives in the beautiful town of Chipley in North Florida. Chipley is a great place to live, but it is not growing quickly, so values increase moderately.

Jim learned the markets in the coastal towns an hour south of his town. He began buying in areas that demanded higher rents and were enjoying significant growth and property appreciation. He put some miles on his car buying and managing these properties, but the difference in profit compensated him well for his time.

Another reason to buy out of town is the opposite of Jimmy's reason. Maybe you live in a town where property has appreciated so rapidly that you cannot afford to buy there with the down payment that you have.

All property, regardless of the price, produces positive cash flow if you don't borrow too much against it. A free and clear house can produce a lot of cash flow. The cash flow it produces may repay a 70 percent or even an 80 percent loan, depending on the terms. If you borrow too much against a house, the cash flow will switch from positive to negative.

In 1976, in Orange County California, you could buy a three-bedroom, two-bath home in a nice subdivision for about $50,000. At that time, this was one of the more expensive housing markets in the country. Today, the same home is selling for about $500,000, and it's still one of the more expensive housing markets in the country.

My students who began buying in southern California in the 1970s and continued throughout the 1980s and 1990s are some of my wealthiest students. With just 20 houses, they control $10 million worth of property. That's 10 times the money you would control with the same houses in many other states.

If you buy that $500,000 house today and rent it for about $2,500 a month, you can only finance about $300,000 and have positive cash flow (payments would be $2,000 with a 30-year 7 percent loan). Thus, to afford that house, you have to put $200,000 down, or buy it below the market and put less down, or finance all or part of it at a better rate, or bring an investor in, or any one of the other strategies I've mentioned in this book.

However, even if you live in Newport Beach, California, you can drive 60 miles and be in a town that has houses that sell for $150,000, that rent for $1,000 a month, and that still appreciate at a better than average rate. Soon those houses will be more expensive. In California, you have to get up early in the morning to make that 60-mile drive in an hour, but it can be done.

BUY PROPERTY IN AN AREA TO WHICH YOU PLAN TO MOVE

Another good reason to buy in another town is to get a foothold in another appreciating market. Florida is about half owned by people who plan on moving there one day. They come on vacation, see the sun in the middle of January, and fall in love.

Buying where you want to move gives you a hedge against rising property values. You want to buy as little management responsibility as possible because you may live a long way away. The cost of a plumber increases directly with the distance you are from the plumber. My friend David Tilney lives in one town near me about half a year but manages his properties in another town half a continent away. He has a cellphone with a local number (in the town where his properties are located), and his tenants and repairers never know that he has left town. This saves him a lot of money.

Many people have tried buying condominiums because of the built-in management. The right condo in the right complex may be a good investment. If you are a condo buyer, you need to understand that the current owners, who run the association, and the condominium manager have an impact on your ability to rent and resell. Spend time talking to the locals (ones not trying to sell you a condo) to get the inside scoop before you buy. Avoid buying in poorly managed complexes or in ones which are unfriendly to investors.

I've decided to rent vacation homes whenever I take a vacation. I prefer to go different places every year, and when I go, I don't want the responsibility of ownership. I am fortunate to live in an area where houses appreciate, so I can make my money at home and then spend it on vacations.

POOR REASONS TO BUY OUT-OF-TOWN PROPERTY

Sometimes we rationalize our decisions using faulty logic. It's easy to get caught up in the moment while you are sunning yourself on a tropical beach or soaking up the crystal clear air at a mountain resort.

When you find yourself excited about a glamorous property, force yourself to go through a cooling off period before you sign a contract. If it's really a great deal, it will still be a great deal in a week after you have had a chance to think through the numbers and compare it with alternative investments.

Another faulty thought is that because the property will be far away, you won't have to think about it, and someone else will do all the work. There is an ad for a brokerage firm that says, "We manage money for people who don't like to think about their money." I'll tell you: If you don't think about your money, you will never have much.

It's a fallacy to think that you won't worry about a house because it's a thousand miles away. A fellow in California owns houses in Houston. They are empty, and he worries about them every day—enough to consider moving to Texas to solve the problem.

I once bought houses in 10 states because I wanted to be in a distinguished real estate society, and to be a member, you had to own property in 10 states. It would have been far cheaper to join the most expensive country club in town.

And the final reason not to buy—because everyone else is doing it. Your big-talking friends may be buying property out of town, but that does not mean that they are making money doing it. In fact, most people who are making a lot of money doing something keep it to themselves. Don't follow the big talkers. They often have small bank balances.

CHALLENGES

There are two major challenges to owning property out of town. The first is getting good information about values and trends. You can go to a town and walk the streets and look at properties that sold recently and get a feel for values. However, without living there, it's hard to get a good feel for the market.

I owned a house in a far-away state with a good friend who was a pro in the business. I put up the money, and he managed the property. We held it for a number of years without seeing much appreciation. One day we got an offer for more than we paid for it; after some discussion, we accepted it. The next couple of years the house skyrocketed in value.

Because I was an out-of-towner, I did not have a feel for the market and missed the big run-up in value.

The second and biggest challenge is finding good management at an acceptable cost. Note that I did not say cheap management. Good management is rarely cheap, and managers who will work cheap are even more rarely good.

PAYING MANAGERS

Ideally, you want a manager who will stay with you for as long as you own the property. You want one who will make good decisions that will make the property both produce income and appreciate. If the manager defers maintenance to increase the cash flow, it may depress the value of the house.

When you pay a manager based only on the gross cash that she is able to generate, that person is tempted to rent to the tenants who will pay the most. Five college kids will pay more rent than a family of four. If the manager makes more money renting to five college kids, you will get five college kids. What will that do to your maintenance expenses? They will be higher, but the manger is paid based on the gross income, not the net—after replacing and repairing all the damage caused by your rowdy tenants.

PAYING YOUR MANAGER A PERCENTAGE OF THE PROFIT YOU MAKE

Once you locate a manager who is good at what he does, make him this offer. Rather than paying him just a little as the cash flow comes in, you keep the cash flow and pay him by giving him half your profit when you sell the house.

Suppose that a house is worth $140,000 today, and you commit to hold it until it doubles in value. When you sell it for $280,000 in the future, your manager would make $70,000, and you would keep the rest. In the transpiring years, you would benefit from all the cash flow, and the manager would have the incentive of trying to keep the house and the neighborhood in good shape to increase the appreciation potential.

If the manager is smart and oriented to the long term, he will do the math. A profit of $70,000 is far better than a commission check of about $120 a month, even if it takes 10 years to collect. You can secure this agreement by giving your manager an option to buy an undivided one-half interest in the house for one-half of today's value.

This is a better deal financially for the manager than it is for you, but having a good manager on the payroll for 10 years without writing him a check is valuable to you. Long-distance management can be very expensive. Think about the man from California I mentioned earlier. He owns two empty houses in Texas. What has it cost him so far to have poor management? What could it cost him over the next 10 years? Some out-of-town owners are so desperate to sell that they sell for less than what they paid, even in a good market. Look for such opportunities, but be careful not to become one.

PAYING TENANTS INSTEAD OF OUT-OF-TOWN MANAGERS

As an alternative, you may consider paying tenants to manage themselves. How? Simply by giving them a break on the rent if they do two things: pay on time and take care of the maintenance on the house. If you have to call somebody to fix something, then they have to pay more rent.

It's the same system I use to rent all my houses and have used for nearly 30 years. It works great, but first you have to find the tenants. This is a challenge to accomplish from a distance.

A solution may be to use a property manager to find you a tenant and pay a one-time fee for that service. Then you talk with your new tenants, explaining the system to them to make sure that they understand it. Have them either deposit the money directly into a local account you set up just for that purpose or have them send the rent directly to you.

THE FINAL WORD

After more than 30 years of experimenting with owning property all over the country, I have concluded that the property I own in my town makes me more money with less aggravation than property in far-away places. I am still tempted, and I might buy property again out of town. However, I will acknowledge when I do that my motivation will be something other than making the greatest profit I can on my investment.

If you live in a growing town with a decent rental market and appreciating property values, resist the temptation to buy in a far-away place. My California friends who have bought in Mississippi, Nevada, Texas, and even Florida typically have been disappointed with the results. Why leave a market you know that performs well for an unknown outcome?

20

Making It Big on Little Deals

In 1976 I began teaching others how to buy houses for investment in a class entitled, "Making It Big on Little Deals." I still teach it twice a year. Many of my students have made it very big. Some own hundreds of houses. Others have bought a few houses to supplement or replace the income from their jobs.

To make money as an investor, you have to take risks. If the risk is small—if it is a little deal—then you are more likely to take it. A modestly priced house in a good neighborhood is almost a risk-free investment. You can buy it with a relatively small down payment and rent it to a tenant who will pay you enough to repay your loan.

It takes a modest amount of work to find, buy, and rent a house, but the reward is more than worth the work and risk. Those who fail to take this chance, who will not make the effort to buy even a safe investment, run a far greater risk—the risk of never building any wealth. The great majority of people, even in our free and wealthy country, do not build any significant wealth. They must rely on the government, a company pension, or relatives for support.

You reduce your risk by learning before you write a check to buy your first investment. Hopefully, this book has answered some of your questions and given you the direction that you need to write that first check and buy that first house.

WRITING DOWN YOUR PLAN FOR BUILDING WEALTH

Commit today to buying at least one house. Use my 10/10/10 rule, and you will own a house that should rent for at least the amount of your payments. You will learn a lot and build some self-confidence in the process.

Now hold onto that house until it doubles in value. Don't refinance it along the way, and your cash flow from that house will increase every year.

All you need to do to become wealthy is to repeat the process, to buy one house a year for 10 years and to hold them until they double in value (see Table 20.1).

If houses in your town double in value every 10 years, Table 20.2 shows what your houses will look like in 10 years if the first house you bought was worth $150,000. (If they don't double in 10 years, hold them until they do.) Your first house will double in value from $150,000 to $300,000, and as you will continue to buy the same type of house in the same neighborhood, all your houses will be worth about $300,000 in 10 years, or when they double.

There is nothing complicated about this plan. It simply requires you to stick with it and buy one house a year and then hold onto those houses until they double in value. These numbers are conservative. As you improve your buying and borrowing skills, you will make deals better than 10/10/10.

SECRETS OF SUCCESS

Warren Buffet has made billions of dollars as an investor during my lifetime. He has done it following some simple guidelines:

Buy value. Buy investments that have real value, and buy them at a bargain price. Buy a house you know the value of that produces income, and buy it when you can make a good deal.

Hold onto your good investments—forever. Don't sell a house that rents well and appreciates. It is making you a lot of money.

Treat others as you would like to be treated. You can make a lot of money buying, renting, and selling houses without ever making anyone mad. When you treat people well, they will send you their friends.

Table 20.1 My Net Worth in 10 Years If I Buy Just One House

1. Market value of the first house you buy today: $__________
2. Using 10/10/10 buy at least 10% below the market: $__________
   - Put no more than 10% down: $__________
   - Your original loan balance: $__________
   - Your beginning equity in the house: $__________
3. Hold your first house until it doubles in value: Line 1 × 2 = $_____
4. The loan balance after 10 years on a 30-year loan is about 86% of the original balance: $__________
5. Your equity (value – loan balance): $__________

An Example with a House Worth $150,000 Today

Here is an example using a house worth $150,000 today:

1. Market value of the first house you buy today: $150,000
2. Using 10/10/10, buy at least 10% below the market: $135,000
   - Put no more than 10% down: $13,500
   - Your original loan balance: $121,500
   - Your beginning equity in the house: $28,500
3. Hold your first house until it doubles in value: Line 1 × 2 = $300,000
4. The loan balance after 10 years on a 30-year 7% loan is about 86% of the original balance: $104,000
5. Your equity (value – loan balance): $196,000

Table 20.2 My Net Worth If I Buy One House a Year for 10 Years

Year	House Price in 10 Years	Approximate Loan Balance in 10 Years	Your Equity in 10 Years
1	$300,000	$104,000	$196,000
2	$300,000	$121,000	$179,000
3	$300,000	$138,000	$162,000
4	$300,000	$155,000	$145,000
5	$300,000	$172,000	$128,000
6	$300,000	$189,000	$111,000
7	$300,000	$206,000	$94,000
8	$300,000	$223,000	$77,000
9	$300,000	$235,000	$65,000
10	$300,000	$245,000	$55,000
Totals	$3,000,000	$1,788,000	$1,212,000

There is unlimited opportunity to build wealth. Buying houses, one at a time, and holding them until they at least double in value can build you more wealth than 98 percent of your friends and neighbors and can do it faster than you can believe.

Take a risk on a little deal—and MAKE IT BIG!

21

HABITAT FOR HUMANITY: HELPING OTHERS BUILD WEALTH, ONE HOUSE AT A TIME

The poor need capital, not charity.

MILLARD FULLER, CO-FOUNDER HABITAT FOR HUMANITY

I discovered the work of Habitat for Humanity when its cofounder, Millard Fuller, spoke to a group in our church in 1985. Millard and Linda Fuller are remarkable people. Millard is an entrepreneur's entrepreneur. He built a successful business while attending law school and achieved financial independence at an early age. Together, Millard and Linda decided that there is more to life than just making money, and they did something truly remarkable. They gave away all the money they had made and dedicated their lives to helping others. They took this action when they were young adults, in their 30s, with four young children to raise.

They founded Habitat for Humanity in 1976. Since then, Habitat has motivated millions of volunteers to share their wealth and talents to help their less fortunate neighbors to build their own homes. Habitat is a partnership between those who need a house and those who are willing to help them get one. It is not a give-away program. Potential homeowners work side by side with volunteers helping to build their homes—and the homes of other Habitat families. Then the homeowners pay for their homes with an affordable interest-free mortgage.

Building wealth one house at time is not the stated mission of Habitat for Humanity. Habitat's mission is to eliminate poverty housing, and it does that by building homes in partnership with families in need, one house at a time. As Habitat volunteers all around the world build houses, it is building wealth for those families.

Before I discovered Habitat for Humanity, I rented to low-income tenants who desperately needed a home. Renting to people who often have to choose between buying food and paying rent is a tough business. I learned quickly that I did not have the heart to make people make that choice. I would go broke managing low-income rentals because I would tell them to buy food or medicine for their children and pay me when they could.

Habitat has provided an opportunity for me, and many others who are fortunate enough to own their own homes to help our hard-working low-income neighbors to build and own their own homes.

Habitat for Humanity is founded on a simple concept: Rather than delegating to government the responsibility for housing the poor, housing that is expensive to build and maintain, Habitat solves the problem permanently by helping people in need of housing build and buy their own homes.

Providing decent housing for the poor in a community dramatically improves that community. Well-housed students perform better in school. Well-housed employees are healthier, happier, and more productive at work. Habitat homeowners take a great deal of pride in their homes and take good care of them. Homeowners become involved in their community and take responsibility. They pay taxes and fight for issues that affect their community.

The proof that this formula works is the high percentage of Habitat homeowners who are flourishing. More than 95 percent of Habitat homeowners are repaying their loans successfully. Considering that these are low-income families, this record of success is nothing less than remarkable.

Habitat is a nondenominational Christian organization that welcomes people of all faiths—or no faith at all—to join in eliminating the blight of poverty housing from our communities. In the richest nation in the world, it should be unacceptable for children to grow up in unhealthy, unsafe housing.

Habitat has grown from building its first house in 1978 to completing homes for more than 180,000 families through 2004. Today Habitat is building homes in 3,000 communities in 100 countries.

Volunteering for Habitat has helped me to understand that each of us can change the world, one family at a time. Every Habitat home is a life-changing experience both for the families who live in the home and for the volunteers who help to build it.

Habitat can be a family adventure. Each of my three children has organized and built a Habitat home in our town by organizing church and school youth groups. Habitat provides an opportunity for you and your children to learn the joy of helping others. Through Habitat's Global Village Program, you can combine a family vacation with a volunteer experience that you will always remember. I encourage you to become involved. For current information on Habitat and how you can get involved in eliminating poverty housing in your town, contact Habitat for Humanity International at www.Habitat.org, or call your local affiliate. Look under Habitat for Humanity in your local phonebook.

Contact Information for Habitat for Humanity, International:

Habitat for Humanity International
121 Habitat Street
Americus, GA 31709-3498
U.S.A.
(229) 924-6935
1-800-Habitat
www.Habitat.org

Index

Index

Index

Index

Index

About the Author

John Schaub has successfully avoided holding a job since graduating from the University of Florida in 1970. He has prospered as a full time single-family landlord and shares what he has learned with other investors through his newsletter and twice-a-year seminars.

He likes spending money as much as making it. John is an instrument rated pilot and has piloted his own plane since 1973, and loves to sail, fish, ski, and travel with his family.

John is an advocate for affordable housing and has served for 18 years on the Board of Habitat for Humanity Sarasota, Inc. and 7 years on the Board of Habitat for Humanity International, Inc. He encourages others to get involved in providing affordable housing.

In the seminars John teaches, students actually find and make offers to purchase houses at wholesale prices. For a schedule of John's courses and a copy of his newsletter go to www.Johnschaub.com, call 800-237-9222, or write to John Schaub at 2677 South Tamiami Trail, Suite 4, Sarasota, FL 34239.